JOURNEY TO
FREEDOM

MANUAL

YMCA OF
MIDDLE TENNESSEE
/SCOTT REALL

NELSON IMPACT
A Division of Thomas Nelson Publishers
Since 1798

www.thomasnelson.com

JOURNEY TO FREEDOM MANUAL

Published by Nelson Impact, a Division of Thomas Nelson, Inc., P.O. Box 141000, Nashville, Tennessee, 37214.

Unless otherwise indicated, all Scripture quotations are taken from the New Century Version®. Copyright © 1987, 1988, 1991 by Word Publishing, a Division of Thomas Nelson, Inc. Used by permission. All rights reserved.

Scripture quotations marked KJV are taken from the King James Version of the Bible.

Scripture quotations marked NKJV are taken from *The Holy Bible*, The New King James Version. Copyright © 1979, 1980, 1982, 1992, Thomas Nelson, Inc., Publishers.

Scripture quotations marked NIV are taken from *The Holy Bible*, New International Version®. Copyright © 1973, 1978, 1984 by International Bible Society. Used by permission of Zondervan Bible Publishers. All rights reserved.

To find a YMCA near you, please visit the following websites:
United States of America: www.ymca.com/
Canada: www.ymca.ca/eng_findy.htm
Trouvez votre YMCA: www.ymca.ca/fre_findy.htm
England: www.ymca.org.uk/home/directory/default.asp
Australia: www.ymca.org.au

Visit www.restoreymca.org for more information on Restore, a life-changing ministry of the YMCA.

ISBN 1-4185-0555-2

Printed in the United States of America.

06 07 08 09 10 VG 9 8 7 6 5 4 3 2 1

CONTENTS

Introduction: The Journey to Freedom   v

WEEK ONE: BEGINNING THE JOURNEY TO FREEDOM

Day 1 – Your Life So Far   3

Day 2 – The Life You Want   9

Day 3 – Finding Hope   16

Day 4 – Real Change Occurs in Three Areas   23

Day 5 – Hidden Prisons: Breaking Free from Bondage   30

Day 6 – Facing the Need for Change   36

WEEK TWO: HIDDEN PRISONS: LIFE-CONTROLLING ISSUES

Day 7 – Breaking the Chain of Negative Thoughts   45

Day 8 – Overcoming a State of Fear   50

Day 9 – Denial and Procrastination   55

Day 10 – Silencing the Inner Critic   61

Day 11– Addictive Thinking   67

Day 12 – Journey to a Life of Peace   72

WEEK THREE: CREATING CHANGE

Day 13 – Universality: You're Not Alone   79

Day 14 – Icebergs: Hitting Our Problems Head-On   84

Day 15 – The Motivation of Change   88

Day 16 – Do It Now: Living the Dash   92

Day 17 – Discarding Old Baggage   97

Day 18 – Relationships on the Journey   103

WEEK FOUR: HOPE RESTORED

Day 19 – Getting Free of a Shameful Life   111

Day 20 – The Pursuit of God   117

Day 21 – A Case of Mistaken Identity   123

Day 22 – Courage Is Our Greatness   128

Day 23 – The Promise of Hope   133

Day 24 – Reformation versus Transformation   140

WEEK FIVE: OVERCOME OBSTACLES

Day 25 – The Power of Small Groups   147

Day 26 – Emotions: Can We Trust Them?   151

Day 27 – Living by Vision and Not by Need   157

Day 28 – Progress, Not Perfection   163

Day 29 – Giving Yourself Permission to Start Again   168

Day 30 – Desire to Be Set Free   174

WEEK SIX: FINISH STRONG

Day 31 – Grieving the Past So You Can Reach for the Future   181

Day 32 – Take a Risk: Step Out of the Boat   186

Day 33 – Perseverance: The Strength to Finish the Race   190

Day 34 – The Struggle for Freedom   195

Day 35 – Blueprint to Freedom: Designing Your Personal Plan of Change   199

Day 36 – Personal Commitment to the Action Plan: You Can Do It!   205

Notes   208

A History of YMCA in America: Building, Sharing, Nurturing for 150 Years   214

Resources That Will Help You on the Journey to Freedom   216

INTRODUCTION

Everyone desires a lifetime of hope, health, and happiness. And in some ways, we all believe we haven't attained it. We long for areas of our life to change. We long for freedom—freedom from our addictions, freedom from worry, freedom from debt, freedom from overeating, or freedom to choose a different career, even if it means we have to go back to school. All of us seek a happy life. But many of us don't know how to begin to find it. Too many obstacles have blocked our way. We've made mistakes. Regrets have formed. Escape led to nowhere. Blaming others only entrapped us more. We all eventually reach a place of exhaustion and need a new vision for life.

This book is a tool designed to help you contemplate change. Psychiatrist and spiritual counselor Gerald May writes, "How much can I respect myself if I do not even know what I really want?"[1] Contemplation is how we get an idea of the life we've always wanted. This is a difficult task to accomplish alone. We need a guide. We need a way to pinpoint the broken areas, the areas in need of change. This is the purpose of *Journey to Freedom*. It will guide you to a new life and provide some answers as to why life has not turned out the way you'd planned. Suggestions will be made. But self-examination is how you'll get the most out of this study. The Bible says, "If you want to build a tower, you first sit down and decide how much it will cost, to see if you have enough money to finish the job. If you don't, you might lay the foundation, but you would not be able to finish."[2] This book is a blueprint that will assist you in counting the cost of change. The last thing we want is for you to lay a foundation of change and then run out of steam before reaching your goals. So we created this book to help you get off to a strong start on your journey to freedom.

The YMCA has been fortunate to be involved in great programs of change. YMCA staff invented basketball and volleyball. The first pro-football team was organized at the YMCA. Bodybuilding, racquetball, Father's Day, the Gideons, Toastmasters, softball, swimming and aquatics, group child care, and the Boy Scouts of America have all been either started at the YMCA or influenced by it. This is why I collaborated with the YMCA to establish Restore Ministries as a core outreach program of the YMCA of Middle Tennessee. I knew the combined efforts for change would result in hundreds of changed lives, and it has. Restore has grown from just 50 participants in the year 2000 to over 2,000 to date. Regardless of the participants' issues, they established boundaries, defeated obsessions, improved their relationships, regained hope, and grew stronger in spirit.

Parts of the study will combine Restore's process of change with the events that led to the invention of basketball at the YMCA training school in Springfield, Massachusetts, the invention of volleyball at the YMCA in Holyoke, Massachusetts, and the invention of racquetball in 1950 at the Greenwich, Connecticut, YMCA. But this is not a history book. It's about change. It's about your life: It's a blueprint to build a new beginning. This revolutionary program of change contains six weeks with six days in a week for a total of 36 days.

Dr. James Prochaska, author of *Changing for Good*, believes there are six well-defined stages of change: pre-contemplation, contemplation, preparation, action, maintenance, and termination. For the next six weeks, we will focus on the first three stages—pre-contemplation, contemplation, and preparation. Only 20 percent of people with problems are ready to change, but more than 90 percent of behavior change programs are solely for those 20 percent of people already prepared to move forward.[3] Because of that, this book is about contemplating change. For the next six weeks, we'll do nothing but contemplate how to change, when to change, what to change, and where change needs to occur, and at the end of the six weeks, you can decide to continue the journey by writing a Plan of Action for your new life. Or you can decide to keep the life you have. The choice is yours. So relax. You're contemplating a journey to freedom. Listen to your spirit, your mind, your body. Let them lead you to a new vision for life.

—SCOTT REALL, Director of Restore Ministries,
a life-changing ministry of the YMCA

BEGINNING THE JOURNEY TO FREEDOM

YOUR LIFE SO FAR

Luther Gulick, physical-education instructor at the YMCA training school in Springfield, Massachusetts, stood at his office window and looked across the school grounds covered with a blanket of decaying autumn leaves. It was December 1891. Bare trees shivered in the north wind, and Gulick knew the eighteen rugby-loving men he would be in charge of over the winter would despise his indoor games. They hated the games of Leapfrog and Drop the Handkerchief. They were tired of tumbling inside while snow fell on icy creeks. They needed stimulation, something to keep them from going stir crazy. So, Gulick challenged James Naismith and other physical-education instructors to develop new indoor games. He gave them two weeks, which would be a daunting task for even the likes of Hasbro. But Naismith jumped at the challenge and tried combinations of several games, mixing and matching them. Nothing seemed to work. Then he remembered a rock-throwing game he'd played in childhood. Maybe he could come up with some variation of it. He doodled out a diagram, placing two goals at each end of the second-level running track. He felt he might have something, so he quickly summoned the school janitor and asked for two boxes. He was going to fasten each box to the second-level running track at opposite ends. But the janitor couldn't find boxes and brought back two half-bushel peach baskets. So, Naismith decided this would have to do, and the janitor secured

3

SPIRIT

"The men where you live," said the little prince, "raised five thousand roses in the same garden—and they do not find in it what they are looking for." "They do not find it?" I replied. "And yet what they are looking for could be found in one single rose or in a little water." "Yes, that is true," I said, and the little prince added: "But the eyes are blind. One must look with the heart . . ."

—ANTOINE DE SAINT-EXPUÉRY, THE LITTLE PRINCE

them at opposite ends. Then he divided the eighteen men into two teams and tacked thirteen rules of the game to the wall. After each goal, the janitor lugged out the ladder and retrieved the ball. This is how the staff at the YMCA invented basketball.

Luther Gulick and James Naismith believed in the possibility of new indoor games. They focused on the solution instead of the problem.

The first goal on the journey to freedom is to believe in the possibility of change. Everyone has the potential to secure a lifetime of hope, health, and happiness. Change is available to everyone. The future can be different. And maybe you are staring into a difficult situation. Maybe you feel like a bare tree shivering in the winter of discontent. Like Gulick, you know something needs to change. But the journey to freedom can be confusing. There are so many remedies and philosophies of change. How do you find the one that's right for you?

The first stage of finding the right program or philosophy is pre-contemplation. You need to know where to apply the process of change. Maybe you need to lose weight or change jobs or stop being an approval addict. Maybe you need to overcome regret. Perhaps you've hit a dead end and you are completely confused. You only know something needs to change. This is okay. Pre-contemplation is the spadework. But pre-contemplation of change cannot happen unless we first believe in the possibility of change.

ANGEL IN THE STONE

One day Pope Julius II watched Michelangelo hammering away at a slab of marble. "Why are you working so hard?" he asked. Michelangelo replied,

"Can't you see there's an angel imprisoned in this block of stone? I'm working as hard as I can to set him free." Inside us is the person we were meant to be. We only need to chip away the parts that keep us in bondage to fear, to addictions, to low self-esteem, to feeling unworthy to be loved by God and others. Change is what happens when we break free from these hindrances. But we have to believe in the possibility of change before we can be set free. Your interest in this book is evidence that you desire change. Somewhere inside, possibility still exists. This is a good thing. You are going to be okay. Change is possible. See yourself as stone and God as the sculptor who is working to set you free. We only need to remain still and let God chip some things away. Yes, it will be painful. Yes, it will be difficult. Unlike the stone, we will feel it. But we have to trust the process. We have to ask tough questions: "What holds me in bondage? What areas of my life need change? Why do I feel hopeless?" These questions will arise during the process of change, but don't feel broken beyond repair. Psychiatrist and spiritual counselor Gerald May says that when we fail at managing ourselves, we feel defective.[1] We all feel like this at times, but it shouldn't hold us back from believing in the possibility of change.

When the Israelites were standing before the Red Sea and Pharaoh was closing fast behind them—trapping them between the two—Moses said to the Israelites, "Don't be afraid! Stand still . . . You only need to remain calm; the LORD will fight for you" (Exod. 14:13–14). The possibility of victory was the first thing God communicated to them. He wanted them to know that freedom was available. To be still in the present and wait requires hope and a sense of promise for the future. This is the essence of change. Possibility abounds.

The second goal on the journey to freedom is to realize we need help. If Gulick's thoughts of possibility led to Naismith's invention of basketball, then our belief in possibility can lead us to the One who can invent change in our life. Saint Augustine once said that God is always trying to give good things to us, but our hands are too full to receive them. Put another way, God is always trying to produce change in us, but we can't stop worrying long enough to receive it.

Worry is the enemy of change. We worry that we will not be able to change. We worry about not being worthy of change. We worry that change will broadcast our faults to the world. But as long as we are in bondage to worry, we will never grasp for the possibility of change. Gulick did not despair over the state of the eighteen rugby-loving men he'd have to play Drop the Handkerchief with that winter. He focused on finding an answer to the problem. Instead of worrying himself into despair, he cleared his mind, so he could do as Oswald Chambers said, "Let God's truth work in you by soaking in it, not by worrying into it. Obey God in the thing He is at present showing you, and instantly the next thing is opened up."

This seems to be how it happened for Luther Gulick and James Naismith. They believed in the possibility of change. Then they did what God was showing them in the moment. For Gulick it was to commission physical-education instructors to come up with new game ideas. He needed outside help. Sometimes it takes others to get us further on the journey to freedom. Freedom is found in numbers: "An enemy might defeat one person, but two people together can defend themselves; a rope that is woven of three strings is hard to break" (Eccles. 4:12). Those who bind themselves together conquer foes, because two are better than one. And when everything within us says, *You can do this alone*, be careful. Secrecy is enslavement, and if enslavement is the result of doing it alone, let's tell someone so we can be free. We can overthrow secret thoughts of despair, destruction, and addiction. But we have to come out of hiding. We need true friends. We need the help of others.

The third goal on the journey to freedom is to make the process of change concrete, instead of a theory. There are many who can talk the theory of change, but somewhere change has to be made in concrete steps. Gulick wanted indoor games to change, so he took a concrete step and challenged those around him to invent new ones. This is pre-contemplation at the beginning of the journey.

We must consider, do we want to take concrete steps toward change? Christ asked the same question of the paralyzed man at the Pool of Bethesda. He asked, "Do you want to be made well?" (John 5:6 NKJV) He did not doubt the man's sincerity. He'd been lying by the pool for thirty-eight years. The paralytic man thought he wanted to be made well, but Christ was asking something different. In essence, He was saying, "A healing will change your life. You will have to get a job to support yourself. You will have to learn a new way of life." Christ was not questioning the theory of healing, but the concrete steps he'd have to take to enjoy his freedom. At some point, healing and growth require concrete steps. This is the opportunity set before you. This has been your life so far, but it can change. Look upon the next six weeks as a challenge. Just as Gulick challenged Naismith to invent new games, come up with a new game plan for your life. The journey to a lifetime of hope, health, and happiness begins when we say, "I want to change. I want to be made well."

REFLECTIONS

CHANGING OUR LIVES BEGINS BY FIRST BELIEVING THAT CHANGE IS POSSIBLE!

- How long have you been thinking about changing your life?

- If you could change anything in your life, what would it be?

- How would you respond if Christ asked you personally, "Do you want to be made well?"

THE LIFE YOU WANT

The students at the YMCA training school in Springfield, Massachusetts loved basketball so much they took it back to their hometowns during Christmas break, and the game began to spread like wildfire. On January 15, 1892, Naismith published the first official basketball rules, and an indoor winter sport was born. Women quickly picked up the game—local schoolteachers were the first to play. The first "official" women's team was formed a year later, with Naismith's future wife among the players. With this kind of phenomenal growth came changes.

When we think about basketball today, we think of dunking; we think of Michael Jordan as he double-clutches the ball and slams it home. We think of the three-point line and zone defense. We think of March Madness and the NBA playoffs. But in the beginning, basketball was rugged, with inept rugby players who had to learn a different type of ball handling. And for the life of them, they couldn't remember the thirteen rules that Naismith posted on the wall. We can picture all eighteen men, plus Naismith and the janitor, huddled around the thirteen rules, trying to deal with a dispute. Probably some of the men questioned a foul or the way someone was handling the ball. Knowing human nature as we do, some may have felt they could come up with better rules. There are know-it-alls in every group. But if we could have attended the very first basketball game, we would have noticed their lack of ability. They weren't very good. The local high-school junior-varsity team would have given those eighteen rugby-loving men a run for their money. The first game, which consisted of two fifteen-minute halves with five minutes of rest between, ended with the score of 1–0. They stunk. They couldn't hit the broad side of a barn. They needed practice. They needed to learn the rules.

So it is with all of us who attempt change. In the beginning, we'll stink. We'll need practice. We'll take the proverbial one-step forward and two steps back. The harder we try, it will seem, the harder change becomes. Expect this. No one masters their problem areas overnight. "No one ever saw a country begin in one day; no one has ever heard of a new nation beginning in one moment" (Isaiah 66:8). We must never demand "overnight delivery" of ourselves. We are not a package headed for Pittsburgh. We are on a journey to freedom. It takes discipline and trial and error. So keep this in mind. Give yourself room to fail.

In her book, *The Writing Life,* Annie Dillard writes that the life expectancy of a crop-duster pilot is five years. "They fly too low. They hit buildings and power lines. They have no space to fly out of trouble, and no space to recover from a stall."[1]

Give yourself room to stall and space to recover. It may take a while to see the results of change. It's like what the Bible says about reaping and sowing. It will take some time to reap the benefits of change. Nothing grows overnight. So, if you don't feel as though you are reaping any benefits, give it some time. Make a spacious place for God to work when you stall. This way you will never crash, because just as the life expectancy of a crop duster is five years, the dropout rate of most programs of change is around 50 percent. To keep yourself out of the negative side of this statistic, leave space for God to work. Don't give up. Change never happens as fast as we'd like. We have to learn the steps, just as the first basketball team had to refer to their rules, so keep coming back to this simple rule: *Change, recovery, growth, and healing are all about hope.*

Hope is a fundamental part of change. Henri Nouwen writes, "Hope is trusting that something will be fulfilled, but fulfilled according to the promises and not just according to our wishes. Therefore hope is always open-ended."[2] Hope believes in spite of the circumstances. Hope is open to change. It is not dedicated to doing the same things over and over again with the same old results. Hope thinks new thoughts.

THE BOTTOM OF THE PEACH BASKETS

In the beginning of basketball, when someone scored a goal, the janitor climbed the ladder, retrieved the ball from the basket, and threw it to a player. Then they carted the ladder off the court. But as the accuracy of the players increased, so did the number of times the janitors had to retrieve the ball. Maybe the janitor spent more time retrieving balls than actually doing maintenance around the school. Who knows? He could have said, "Guys, you are killing me. The better you get, the more time I spend climbing this ladder. Something needs to be done." We don't know how it happened, but someone got the ingenious idea to cut the bottoms out of the peach baskets. This revolutionized the game. They tried something different in hopes of making the game more efficient. Eventually metal rims and cord nets replaced the baskets.

The first goal for today is to concentrate on making life better, not perfect. Avoid the idea that change is a matter of perfection. We are learning new principles to live by, which means we need patience. The reason people drop out of a program of change is because they feel like permanent failures. But remember that mistakes are not fatal. *Problems are only temporary. Circumstances change.* Start a journal. Write down the negative things that you worry will come true. Then go back in six weeks and see how many of them actually took place. We tend to be more fatalistic than we think. Begin to concentrate more on how things can change, instead of worrying about how bad things are.

The second goal for today is to understand the presence of a crisis. Usually we don't change until our problems cause a crisis. For the game of basketball, it was the crisis of wasted time retrieving the ball. In our lives, we begin the process of change when life becomes unmanageable. Our problems dominate our time and energy. We get tired. We reach the point that we just can't face another day of pain. As C. S. Lewis said, pain is God's megaphone. It is a shipwreck of our

11

MIND

"You need to claim
the events of your life
to make yourself
yours."
—ANN WILSON SCHAEF

own making. And to get back to the surface, we must suffer the consequences of our actions. We do this by refusing to involve loved ones. We stop blaming others. We no longer manipulate other people for selfish gain. We cease to run. We face our crisis and take responsibility for it.

Thomas Merton called this the "darkness of the beginning."[3] We become overwhelmed and, in a sense, fall to our knees. We cry out for help from the blackest hole. It's the moment when we cut the bottom out of our peach-basket problems, making way for a revolution in our lives.

When all of our human resources and efforts fail us, we tend to empty our hands so God can fill them with Himself. This happened to me after I suffered through a divorce. I'd reached the end of myself. I struggled with low self-esteem because I felt like a failure. I could not fill the hole in my heart. I'd searched by acquiring worldly possessions. I pursued power. I sought human relationships. I tried sports. I tried writing screenplays and pursued different jobs. Nothing seemed to help. I believed that perhaps a new relationship with a woman could fix me and make me complete so that I would feel good about myself again. Eventually I realized that no other person has the ability to fill the void. I felt hopeless. *I will never change. This is all I will ever know,* I thought as my world began to collapse around me. Then it was as if God called to me, and the only thing I could think to do was get in my car and drive to Percy Warner Park in Nashville, Tennessee.

I've always felt close to God in nature, and I knew I had to get alone with Him. It was fall, and the trees of Tennessee were on fire with dashes of orange and red and the yellows of diminishing green leaves. I parked my car and made my way beneath oaks and ashes, hackberries, locusts, and maples. I heard nothing and saw no one but the leaves as they began their descent, glancing ever so gently off those that remained on the trees. The air was full of them and the ground was blanketed. They crackled beneath my feet as I walked deeper into the woods, searching for a place to collapse on my knees. It was my "darkness of the beginning," the place where I finally cried out to God about the hole in my life, that place of darkness. I wanted to be made well. In the midst of nature's changing season, I fell to my knees and cried for six hours, until nothing remained. It was the beginning of a new life for me.

After that day in the park, I got into a twelve-step program and began the most difficult part of change—self-examination. It was the moment when I cut out the bottom of my peach basket. I tried something different. The same old thing with the same old results had to change, so I stopped looking for fulfillment in a relationship with another person. I learned to love God and be loved by God. Whether we know it or not, this is what we *all* desire. I discovered this in the presence of my crisis.

The third goal for today is knowing where to place the X. There's a great story Clifton Fadiman tells about Charles Steinmatz, an electrical-engineer genius who worked for General Electric in the early part of the twentieth century. On one occasion after his retirement, they called him in because the other engineers were baffled about the breakdown of a complex of machines. They asked Charles to pinpoint the problem. He walked around the machines for a while, then took a piece of chalk out of his pocket and made a big cross mark on one particular piece of one particular machine.

To their amazement, when the engineers disassembled that part of the machine, it turned out to be the precise location of the breakdown.

A few days later, the engineers received a bill from Charles for $10,000—a staggering sum in those days. So, they returned the bill and asked him to itemize it. He returned the bill with a note that read:

Making one cross mark: $1.00
Knowing where to put it: $9,999.00

Changing our lives always starts with putting the cross mark on the right spot. This is the work of pre-contemplation. Gerald May writes, "How much can I respect myself if I do not even know what I really want?"[4] I'll add, "How can I change if I haven't identified the problem?" Pre-contemplation is learning where to look for the problem. A weight problem may be the result of emotional eating due to some overwhelming hurt. An addiction problem may be the result of a deep-seated insecurity. Of course, we could go on describing these kinds of symptoms. But until we perform a self-examination, we will not have a clue about how to change. My guess is that this is the reason most people drop out of groups. Either they feel broken beyond repair, or they don't know why their life is broken. They can point to many things that are wrong, but they do not know where to draw the X. We need outside help. Other people can help us find the spot if we are willing to look. Looking is the key.

This is what Luther Gulick did when he stood at the window. He thought about the eighteen rugby-loving men who did not want to play Drop the Handkerchief. He didn't place the mark on their chests, blaming them for their dissatisfaction. He placed the mark on the fact that the current indoor games were not meeting their needs. He then took the crisis and changed the face of indoor games with the help of James Naismith.

The presence of a crisis may be the beginning of a new life. God loves to redeem shattered lives. He's the source of power to help us on the journey to freedom.

REFLECTIONS

HOPE IS A FUNDAMENTAL PART OF CHANGE.

- Have you ever lost all hope of changing?

- Can you pinpoint your most significant problem?

- Have you ever experienced a moment in life when you've totally surrendered to God?

FINDING HOPE

One of James Naismith's former students, Phog Allen, considered the "father of basketball coaching," told Naismith he was going to Baker University to coach basketball. Naismith said, "Why, basketball is just a game to play. It doesn't need a coach." But the University of Kansas counts Naismith among its coaches. Evidently, he changed his mind about a coaching career and coached basketball there for nine years. The inventor of the game is the only coach in University of Kansas history with a losing record: 53 wins and 55 losses. How embarrassing! The man who invented basketball could not coach his way to a winning record. But to see Naismith as a basketball failure would be a gross injustice. He invented it. He fathered it, in many ways. So his losing record only makes him human. Everyone has good traits and bad ones. Naismith could have been more creative than administrative. Who knows? But he is a great example of how we live with the tension of both failures and successes.

Everyone has failures. Our lives aren't black and white. If we don't win at certain things, it doesn't mean we are permanent failures. We may win next time, or we may lose three more times before we win. But the trap most of us fall into is what psychologists call *disqualifying the positive*, that is, drawing conclusions from only the negative. Naismith could have thought of himself as a failure because of his losing record. But this would have disqualified his positive contribution of inventing basketball.

Everyone has positive things of worth in their lives. Our jobs may be unrewarding, but our children may bring us much joy. To focus only on the negative aspects of our careers is to disqualify the joy of having children. Our financial circumstances may be challenged, but our marriages may be great. To focus only on the finances disqualifies a great relationship. Money can cause problems. But the moment we allow the negatives to ruin the positives, life gets out of balance. Relationships end in turmoil. Jobs become drudgery. But we are never without hope. We can never disqualify God's help. He offers the great possibility of life. The Bible says, "We know that in everything God works for the good of those who love him."[1] God will take bad things and bring something good from them. This is the hope we are looking for—the hope of God's help. Remember, Augustine said that God is always trying to give good things to us, but

> **BODY**
>
> Strength training is the fountain of youth. It maintains or increases our lean muscle mass, which permanently raises our rested metabolic rate, the amount of calories we burn at rest; it maintains or increases our bone mass and helps prevent osteoporosis.

our hands are often too full to receive them. This is what it means to disqualify God's help. We believe life is manageable on our own, so we stick to what we think is working. But in reality, each day moves us closer and closer toward becoming a negative person who gives up on life.

In C. S. Lewis's book, *The Great Divorce,* he deals with the differences between heaven and hell. In this fictional piece, people from earth take a day trip to the bright borders of heaven, where they seem to become ghosts against the brilliance of that place. The narrator embarks on an incredible voyage through heaven and hell, meeting a host of supernatural beings that teach him the nature of good and evil. One ghost wanders into the narrator's path with a little red lizard on his shoulder. The lizard whips its tail back and forth while whispering lustful words into the ghost's ear, tormenting him with thoughts of evil. But when the angel offers to kill the lizard, the ghost says, "Honestly, I don't think there's the slightest necessity for that. I'm sure I shall be able to keep it in order now."

SPIRIT

"When a man is at his wits' end, it is not a cowardly thing to pray; it is the only way he can get in touch with reality."
—Oswald Chambers, My Utmost for His Highest

It seems rational for us to believe that we can keep our own lives in order, just as the ghost in Lewis's story believed he could keep the red lizard in order. Sometimes we can keep our own "lizards" at bay. Sometimes we feel as if we are free of it. But then the whispers begin again. The trap we fall into is trying to maintain the normality of a life that isn't working. We believe we can handle our problems on our own. This is the lie of normality.

The first goal of the day is to end normality. We have to admit that the life we are now leading isn't working. Decide to switch from mere survival to a new way of life.

A recent television program showed a method for trapping monkeys. The natives made a hole in a log and put bait inside. The hole was just big enough to allow the monkey room to get his opened hand inside the log. So, the monkey reached his hand in to get the bait, but when his fingers closed on it, making a fist, he couldn't get his fist back through the hole. Determined to hang on to what he had, he was still there, trapped by his own greed, when captured. We are much like this monkey when we hold on to a life of normality. We fail to do the one thing that would free us, which is to let go and try a new way of life.

The second goal of the day is to identify the traits of our normality so we can begin to eliminate them. Think about the areas of your life that need change. This means even the areas you may think you are managing with normality.

In Day 2, we discussed how our problems are temporary. Now we begin the process of listing the areas where we desire change. This is *not* an action step, but merely a way to get you to think through what can or cannot change in your life. So, take a few minutes and list your problem areas:

The areas in which I desire change are:

1. _____

2. _____

3. _____

4. _____

5. _____

Once you've listed these areas, begin to think about some areas that will never change. Unchangeable areas need pinpointing in the pre-contemplation stage. This way you will not get frustrated and quit with *all-or-nothing thinking,* which is the belief that either our life has to be perfect in every area or it is a failure. Keep in mind that many areas can change for the better, but life will not be a work of perfection. Make peace with this before you begin the journey to freedom. This is the thought behind the Serenity Prayer:

> *God grant me the serenity to accept the things I cannot change; courage to change the things I can; and wisdom to know the difference.*
> —*Reinhold Niebuhr*

The *wisdom to know the difference* is the key. Focus on what can change. So many times we become obsessed with things over which we have no control, such as other people. We cannot control their behavior and make them treat us nicely. Dr. Phil McGraw says that we teach other people how to treat us. So, we can never say that someone won't allow us to change. We are in control of our own behavior.

We can also blame our circumstances. It's easy to say we've tried it all and nothing has worked, and we refuse to give our circumstances a new look. This happened to Jesus' disciples. They had fished all night on the Lake of Galilee and had caught nothing. Early the next morning, Jesus stood on the shore and called out to them, "Friends, did you catch any fish?" They answered, "No." He said, "Throw your net on the right side of the boat, and you will find some." So they did, and they caught so many fish they could not pull the net back into the boat.[2]

The disciples were fishermen by trade. They knew the lake. They knew the shoreline and the depths. They knew all about fishing—what worked and what didn't. But they failed to do one thing. They failed to see the trap of normality. Jesus didn't order them to park the boat and take up a rod and reel. He didn't force them into doing something that contradicted their knowledge of fishing. He only suggested another style—the other side of the boat. This is the God-factor. An old fishing hole becomes a full net. Attain new heights with God's help. Remain open. If you feel shoved into change, you will disqualify the positive and quit.

The goal is to make life better, not perfect. Fight normality, which is the fear of doing life in a different way. If Naismith had feared change, then today's basketball retrieval method would still be climbing a ladder. He could have said, "This is how we play the game. There is no other way." But he was flexible and open to trying something different if it improved the game. This is the decision we make in pre-contemplation. We open our minds to a new kind of life. We make the commitment to think in new ways to improve life.

The third goal of the day is to discover a vision. On Day 2, I told the story of my reaching the end of myself at Percy Warner Park. In that moment, everything was dark. I had no vision. I was too deep in the blackness to see my way out of my circumstances. I needed God's help. It was the "darkness of the beginning." And the important word here is *beginning.* The darkness may have been great in the beginning, but now we need the light. We need vision.

In pre-contemplation, we find the vision that is opposite of the world's, opposite of obtaining wealth, power, and prestige. Society believes happiness is a result of these three things. But just as I thought one more relationship would make me complete, it never did. I found myself exhausted and hopeless. So, we need to begin to think about where we want life to take us from here. This is vision. It's a simple goal, done one day at a time. And the goal of every day is to trust at all times that God is with you and will meet your needs. Finding hope is a matter of trust.

The amazing thing about the story of the disciples' fishing on the other side of the boat is how there were hot coals and fish already on the fire when they reached the shore. Jesus provided breakfast. He had a plan for their day. And the key to hope is to believe every day that Jesus will appear with the resources you need to walk out the new life He calls you to live. Christ's presence brings success. Stay close to Him, and He will bring the power you need. He knows how to guide. He knows where the fish hide. He sees all things. The Bible says, "When you pass through the waters, I will be with you. When you cross rivers, you will not drown. When you walk through fire, you will not be burned, nor will the flames hurt you."[3]

Finding hope involves making new decisions about our old way of life. It's about God's presence on the journey. As Saint Teresa of Avila said, "The feeling remains that God is on the journey, too."

REFLECTIONS:

THE MOMENT WE ALLOW THE NEGATIVES TO RUIN THE POSITIVES, OUR LIVES GET OUT OF BALANCE.

- If you were the trapped monkey, could you let go and escape?

- Do you believe we can control our behavior?

- Do you want a perfect life or a better life?

REAL CHANGE OCCURS IN THREE AREAS

In 1893, basketball developed a huge problem. Overzealous spectators in the balcony were interfering with the game. They'd reach down and knock the ball away from the basket, infuriating the players and endangering the fairness of the game. Something had to be done about the interference. But what? They could not move the spectators out of the balcony or reposition the goals. So, the search for a remedy soon led to the creation of the first backboard, which was made out of wire mesh. And it worked! The backboard defended the goal against the spectators who were impeding the game.

One of the things we will face while trying to change our lives is interference. Numerous self-defeating behaviors can interfere with our process of change. We can undervalue ourselves and be unaware of our inadequacies or the life skills we possess to overcome them. But knowledge can raise awareness and build a wire mesh of protection against these self-defeating behaviors, just as the game of basketball used the backboard to defend the goal from interference. Energy we expend against ourselves will weaken our power to change. It interferes.

There are three interference attitudes that will impede our attempts at change.

"I tried it once, and it didn't work." Many of us attempt change, only to give up after one try. We believe we are what we are and can never change. We try

to quit smoking and fail after only one day. We tell ourselves that we don't have what it takes. We tell ourselves it's impossible. We go on a diet, but after a week of failing to lose any significant weight, we say, "I can't lose weight. There's nothing I can do about it." Others try harder, believing that willpower can change them, but soon they, too, fail.

Even though willpower is an element of change, it is not the deciding factor. The way to overcome the self-defeating behavior of giving up is to train, not try. Training versus trying is the key to success. John Ortberg, in his book *The Life You've Always Wanted,* writes, "Spiritual transformation is not a matter of trying harder, but of training wisely. . . . There is an immense difference between training to do something and trying to do something."[1] When we try to change and do not succeed, we tend to give up after a few attempts. But when we *train* to do something, we set our minds on learning. No matter how many times we fail, we see ourselves as being one step closer to succeeding.

Think of an Olympic athlete. She doesn't just show up and try really hard on the day of her particular event. She trains her spirit, mind, and body long before the Olympics even begin.

Although you may not be an Olympian, training is the key to reaching every goal. A weightlifter progresses toward his goal weight by training his muscles a little at a time. If he fails, he trains his muscles until they exert the power needed to reach the desired goal. Ortberg writes, "Trying hard can accomplish only so much . . . you will have to enter into a life of training."[2] Trying is the raw use of willpower, nothing more. Training is learning the life skills needed for long-term change.

Start where you are with the mindset of training your spirit, mind, and body over the next six weeks. Allow your spirit to be inspired. Learn health tips. Raise the awareness of your mind, so you can train for freedom. This is the success Phil discovered at Restore.

Phil first came to Restore Ministries at the YMCA because he'd *tried hard* to change with willpower and failed. Multiple DUIs and an accident landed him in jail for a year, and during all of this turmoil, he lost his home, business, and fiancée. To make it worse, after being released from jail, he soon received his fifth DUI. This is when Phil hit rock bottom. He came to the realization that alcohol was his downfall. But he wasn't sure another recovery program would help. He'd tried numerous programs and failed. Instead of training and learning from his mistakes, he plunged deeper into a vortex of darkness as he continued to try harder, only to fail. Nothing seemed to work. He felt he would never change.

> **SPIRIT**
>
> It is worth nothing for them to have the whole world if they lose their souls.
> —Matthew 16:26

At Restore, Phil learned that change takes place when we bring into harmony the spirit, mind, and body. And once we helped Phil plug in to the spiritual dimension, he transformed. His mind had been constantly engaged in the act of division from his body and spirit, and as long as this was taking place, he could not change. Psychiatrist and spiritual counselor Gerald May believes that maintaining a healthy balance between the spirit, mind, and body is how we change. He writes, "Both Eastern and Western medical sciences have long understood that maintaining natural balances is the body's greatest priority; if the systems of the body are going to work at all, they must work together in harmony. When equilibrium is thrown off balance, the result is *stress*."[3]

The key in the process of change is to balance the spirit, mind, and body. This has been the YMCA's focus for over a hundred years. Because the YMCA knew early on that even though a person might be a physical specimen of robust health, his or her spirit may be malnourished, and before long there is a disconnect. In Phil's case, he had medicated his mind, but he'd damaged his body and spirit. Anytime we leave out one of the three, it produces stress in the body, low self-esteem in the mind, and displacement in the spirit through our longing for the wrong objects—power, prestige, and possessions.

"Disqualifying the positive." Not only did the backboard defend the game from overzealous spectators, it revolutionized the game on the court, turning a negative into a positive. Players learned to shoot using the backboard. We

> ## SPIRIT
>
> "I saw the angel in stone and carved until I set him free."
>
> —MICHELANGELO

often hear people at a basketball game yell, "Use the board." Now this is good advice, but in 1893, the backboard had only one function—to stop the interference. But later the players discovered that the backboard had multiple positives. It helped their shots and propelled the game forward to become what it is today.

Every situation has a positive element to it that can drive change. The way to overcome negative interference is by eliminating what has been called the *"yeah, but"* syndrome. Let's say your boss gives you the promotion you've longed for, and when someone congratulates you, you say, "*Yeah, but* it means I'll have more responsibilities." Or maybe you lose twenty pounds and someone pays you a compliment, and you respond, "*Yeah, but* I'm not at the weight I was in high school." You may never get back to your high-school weight, so don't disqualify the progress you've made or injure the positive. Any energy we expend disqualifying the positive takes away from our power to change. It interferes.

Martin Seligman, professor of psychology at the University of Pennsylvania, writes in his book, *Learned Optimism*: "Finding temporary and specific causes for misfortune is the art of hope. People who make permanent and universal explanations for their troubles tend to collapse under pressure, both for a long time and across situations."[4] So hope is an integral part of change. If James Naismith had allowed the overzealous spectators to take over the game, their actions could have permanently injured the game. Who knows? But he saw it as a temporary setback that needed a solution, not a detrimental blow to the game of basketball.

Maybe you've hit an obstacle. Something is interfering with your hope, health, or happiness. Is it a temporary setback or a permanent one? If you interpret it as a temporary hindrance, you can discover ways, like Phil did, to overcome it. But if you disqualify the positive, you may feel helpless and hopeless. You may remain stuck in a pattern of defeat. The awareness you can raise is to understand that your problems are temporary. You *can* overcome them.

The third interference is "approval addiction." Everyone desires love and acceptance. This is normal. But when we search for fulfillment in all the wrong relationships, it can disconnect our spirit from God. In his book, *Addictions and Grace*, Dr. Gerald May writes, "[A]ll human beings have an inborn desire for God. Whether we are consciously religious or not, this desire is our deepest longing and our most precious treasure. It gives us meaning."[5]

> ## MIND
>
> "The life which is not examined is not worth living."
>
> —PLATO

The way to block the interference of seeking approval at all costs is to see it for what it is: a need for love and a desire for God, the source of all love and acceptance. Without God's love, it feels as if there is a hole in our soul where life leaks out. We frantically seek to fill this hole with objects of desire, such as addictions, bad relationships, impulsive behavior, and other things that ultimately don't satisfy our craving for God's love. I spent almost my entire life running to different objects. Now I understand the hard truth that as a man, I entered every area of life with an emotional deficit. It was here in total isolation that I felt hopeless. I longed for someone to love and accept me, so I could feel good about myself. But no human or substance can fill the God-shaped hole in our soul.

In the movie *The Last Samurai*, Tom Cruise's character, Nathan Algren, is a great example of a man with a hole in his soul. He had regrets. He wished he could change the horrors of war that haunted him, because somewhere on the unforgiving plains near the banks of the Washita River, Algren's soul was wounded. He became an empty cup with a hole. No matter how hard he tried to fill it with alcohol, it didn't seal the hole. While held captive in a Samurai village, he became severely ill as a result of alcohol withdrawal. He told Katsumoto, the Samurai leader, that he didn't care if he lived or if he died. But during his captivity he was awakened to the hole in his soul and went through a spiritual transformation.

We seek today what Nathan Algren sought—something that will make us feel alive again, something to seal the hole in our soul. For Phil, his drinking never cured his emptiness or set him free. Addictions never fulfill our longings to love and be loved. True fulfillment and purpose seals the hole when we learn to balance the spirit, mind, and body in such a way that they no longer interfere with one another, but complement each other's growth.

Phil plugged in to the spiritual dimension and moved from bondage to freedom. Maybe you need to integrate the exercise of the body into your life to get the desired change you seek. Or maybe you need to integrate the right thoughts by refusing to give up and by rejecting the impulse to disqualify the positive. Maybe you have a hole in your soul and desire to love and be loved by God. Whatever the case, real change occurs in three areas, and when we train in all three areas, the training propels the process of change.

REFLECTIONS

**THE KEY TO THE PROCESS OF CHANGE IS TO
BALANCE OUR SPIRIT, MIND, AND BODY.**

• How do we balance our spirit, mind, and body?

• Do you see change as "training to change" or "trying to change"?

• Do you ever disqualify the positive?

HIDDEN PRISONS:
BREAKING FREE FROM BONDAGE

William Morgan, a YMCA instructor in Holyoke, Massachusetts, felt that basketball was too strenuous for the businessmen at the Holyoke YMCA. He wanted a sport that provided exercise without forcing people to run. So, he blended various elements of other games, strung a badminton net across the gym floor, and brought out the bladder of a soccer ball, birthing a game he named *mintonette*. Probably not the best name given a sport in the history of athletics. It sounds more like an expensive after-dinner mint than the name of a new sport. Think of names for other sports like baseball, football, basketball, and handball. These names clearly point to an aspect of the game and the part of the body involved in playing the sport. But what was this game called *mintonette*?

You may be surprised at what you actually know about *mintonette*. Almost every American has played this sport invented by William Morgan. It became a big hit with the businessmen at the Holyoke Y. But then there was that cumbersome name, a name that didn't fit. And even though Morgan had successfully blended various games to invent *mintonette*, when he tried to name the game by using a variation of the word *badminton*, it just didn't seem to fit. Then one day it all came clear to him during an exhibition game at the

Springfield YMCA Training School, the birthplace of basketball. During the exhibition game, a spectator approached Morgan and commented that the game centered on volleying and should be called "volleyball." Morgan agreed and changed the name.

Morgan realized that combining old names to create a new one did not fit his sport. The beginning of change happens when we question the life we have. Is it adequate? Is it complimenting who we are, or is it distracting us from our purpose here on earth? Sometimes reassessing and renaming our situations can revolutionize us. We see this practice all through the Bible. Patriarchs change their names after a long struggle with their circumstances to describe their new character: "Your name will no longer be Jacob. Your name will now be Israel, because you have wrestled with God and with people, and you have won."[1] The name change is an outward demonstration of an inward change. Jacob overcame his circumstances. He persevered. And what we all hope for at the end of the day is to emerge from our struggles a better person.

Real change transforms our character when we shatter old ways of thinking. We realize we've built our lives upon sand. Now we desire solid rock for a foundation. And the only way to transform is to reinterpret the life we have.

Emotions and memory can work together to construct a powerful matrix of deception. In the movie, *The Matrix,* Morpheus tells Neo that the Matrix is the world that has been pulled over his eyes to blind him from the truth. I believe this kind of matrix can happen in real life. We allow an old way of thinking to dominate our future events. We interpret what we see by what we feel and know from the past. Certain smells cause us to remember where and when we last experienced a certain dish of food, or the tobacco in our grandfather's pipe, or the cologne of a past lover or friend.

Remember the experiment in school where you had to identify a certain piece of fruit placed in your hand while blindfolded. Using everything but

> ## SPIRIT
>
> "God will bring the vision He has given you to reality in your life if you will wait on His timing."
> —OSWALD CHAMBERS,
> *MY UTMOST FOR HIS HIGHEST*

sight, you had to discern the fruit's identity using past experience. Similarly, this is how our minds and emotions interpret present circumstances. We compare them to the past. But the problem is, past experiences can't always interpret future events. To do so is to overgeneralize, which is taking the past and generalizing it to all new events. It's similar to what we discussed on Day 4 about trying it once and concluding that it doesn't work. But overgeneralization moves farther away from just trying one remedy. It generalizes failure to include *all* of life's circumstances—past and present. So, we succumb to the belief that there is no use trying. It's the Popeye syndrome: "I am what I am."

Most of us resist change or we want to discover change on our own terms, like the story of the man trapped in his home by floodwater. As the waters reached his front door, he prayed, "God, please rescue me." Ten minutes later, a boat came by, offering to take the man to safety. "No," said the man, "God will save me." The floods rose, and the man, now trapped upstairs, again prayed, "God, please help me." Five minutes later, another boat came, but again the man declined its help. "God will save me," he said, and the boat went away. At last the flood drove the man to the roof where he prayed, "God, please help me." Almost at once a roaring sound hovered above. The man said, "I don't need a helicopter. God will rescue me." The man drowned. In heaven, he complained to God about not being rescued, and God replied, "I sent two boats and a helicopter!"

Sometimes we hold tight to the wrong life, even when it proves to be detrimental to us. We deceive ourselves by believing a miracle cure will rescue us. Sometimes we interpret outside help as interfering with this miracle. Morgan could have rejected the spectator's advice to name the game *volleyball*. He could have said, "*I* want to name the game. I don't need outside help. The name is what it is, period." By resisting change, he could have prevented volleyball from being the popular sport that it is today.

Accepting change happens when we focus on the solution of a problem more than on our personal comfort. It feels safe not to change. We only need to make sure our resistance is not due to fatalism, because sometimes fatalism creeps in and is interpreted as our fate.[2] But the way out of fatalistic thinking is to reinterpret our circumstances by realizing there is hope, there is a new way of life available to us. We always have choices. Always.

Clara, a sixty-three-year-old grandmother whose arthritis prompted her to join the YMCA of Greater Seattle and participate in its programs, took the first step to reinterpret her life by joining the Y. She says, "Little did I know how it would change my thinking, my habits, and my outlook on health and fitness. My weight started to drop, and after five months, I had shed thirty pounds. My body image totally changed. I'm still a gray-haired, bespectacled granny with a few extra pounds, but I feel energetic, successful at maintaining my weight, able to lose a few pounds if I choose, and confident I can meet any challenge in my life."[3]

Clara challenged her old "matrix" of beliefs that held her in bondage. She broke free. She took control of her weight and destiny by shattering her old ways of thinking and became confident that she could face any challenge in the future. She even lost thirty pounds in the process.

The beauty of the concept of changing spirit, mind, and body is that when we promote change in one area, it affects the other two. Just as Clara joined the Y to benefit from physical exercise, she also reaped a healthier attitude in her mind. We don't have to change everything overnight. Like Clara, we can start with one area, one day at a time. Small steps lead to advancement, no matter what the speed. Believe you can change, and this attitude, coupled with God's strength, will help you form a better way of life. Fate is not our master: God is, and He says, "Come to me, all of you who are tired and have heavy loads, and I will give you rest."[4]

William Morgan believed he could invent a less strenuous game than basketball, and he did. Maybe his first name for the game was horrible. But he didn't worry about the name in the beginning. He concentrated on breaking free from the old matrix to invent a new game. And when the game came into focus, the name changed. And so will your life—one baby step at a time. This is the beauty of change. The only thing required is the desire to have a different life from the one you have now. Breaking free from hidden prisons is done by becoming aware of what binds us to the past. Finding hope to overcome the prison is as simple as discarding everything that tells you that you will never change. All things are possible with God.[5] Freedom occurs when we journey to new destinations that can't be defined by the past.

REFLECTIONS

**REAL CHANGE TRANSFORMS OUR CHARACTER
WHEN WE SHATTER OLD WAYS OF THINKING.**

• Do you feel your life can change for the better?

• Have you ever responded to God's help like the man on his roof did?

• Are you successful at looking for the solutions to problems?

• How do you differ from Clara, the sixty-three-year-old grandmother in this chapter?

FACING THE NEED FOR CHANGE

After surviving a pulmonary embolism, Kristy decided on a lifestyle change. She joined a YMCA in Florida in April 2002 to improve her health, to lose weight, and to keep it off. She weighed over 400 pounds, but Kristy was determined—and scared. She knew her health patterns had to change. So, she began by doing low-impact aerobics twice a week and weight training three times a week. As she started to lose the weight, she added more cardiac exercises (such as biking and using the treadmill and elliptical machines). By November 2003, Kristy had lost 205 pounds! Now she visits the YMCA four times a week to maintain her goal weight and to stay healthy.

Change usually takes place out of developmental or environmental forces that urge us to rethink our condition.[1] All of us reach age milestones or face health conditions that cause us to reevaluate our lives. We ask: Are we healthy? Have we reached our spiritual goals? Do we have a sense of well-being? Usually health threats or age milestones usher us to the point of needing to change.

Here's a list of possible developmental and environmental pressures that frequently bring people to the threshold of change:

- Moving from one stage of life to another (adolescence to adulthood, for example)

- Aging
- Turning forty (most smokers quit at this age)
- Marriage
- Childbirth
- Job dissatisfaction
- A promotion or termination
- Illness
- Life-debilitating addiction
- Retirement
- Inner emotional turmoil
- Death of a loved one
- Divorce
- Health problems
- Societal pressure[2]

> ## SPIRIT
>
> "Keep your life so constantly in touch with God that his surprising power can break through at any point. Live in a constant state of expectancy and leave room for God to come as he decides."
> —OSWALD CHAMBERS, *MY UTMOST FOR HIS HIGHEST*

Some items on this list are the natural result of life, while others are thrust upon us by our own choices. All of them usher in the possibility for change in some capacity. Those who fail to respond properly to environmental and developmental pressures usually repress the need for change. Some alcoholics continue to drink even after a dismal health report. Some smokers are known to smoke even with a tracheotomy. Phil—mentioned in Day 4—knew his drinking had become more than just social, even though he checked the box marked "social drinker" on the health-club application.

What holds most of us back from experiencing change is *fear*. We fear what others will think if, like Kristy, we walk into the Y weighing over 400 pounds. Can you imagine the courage it must have taken for her to face this fear?

We've all had the false belief that YMCAs are for healthy people who are there to simply maintain their great health. But this belief holds us back from change. I wish I could convince people to get involved in change before they

BODY

Everytime I walk into the YMCA, I am motivated because people are swimming, shooting basketball, dancing, lifting weights, and walking. There are people of all ages, races, and walks of life.

are faced with a health scare or developmental or environmental pressure. But the avoidance of change, I believe, stems from low self-esteem.

Low self-esteem is the silent moth that eats away our courage to change. I see this as a certain kind of pessimism. Over all the years we have worked with people at the YMCA and Restore Ministries, we find that the majority of them struggle, at some level, with low self-esteem. They may have life-controlling issues such as addictions, obesity, risky behavior, or even pornography, but underneath there's a deep struggle with low self-esteem.

When low self-esteem sets in, we begin to question our worth when we should be questioning our circumstances. Something is fueling our low self-worth. Sometimes we hate our job, but we're too scared to go and apply for the one we desire, and then we berate ourselves for playing it safe. We could be in an abusive relationship or have too many failures to list in one lifetime. But we have to work at finding our true self, and this may mean a change has to occur.

Most people who face change of any kind have to overcome self-resistance. They feel safe, yet dissatisfied. It's an interesting dichotomy. They feel safe in their addictions or other problems because they know what to expect. And the number-one drawback from change is getting people to take the risk.

If we can raise the awareness about low self-esteem and concentrate on ways to overcome our self-loathing, then we will have a chance at changing. But many of us put on our happy faces and back out of our driveways or take the subway to work, knowing that we are slowly killing the true self we long to become. The paradox of low self-esteem is that we project a false self to protect our true desires that we feel will be rejected if discovered. In essence, we say, "If you really discover who I am at my core and what I long to be, then you'd reject me. Abandon me. Isolate me. Tell me that the life I long for can't be discovered." This is why we hide this inner longing until it comes out in unhealthy ways. We use drugs to alter our moods. We try to live vicariously through the lives of our children. We perform through a false self to gain approval. We have to work at finding our true self, and then change to become who we really are.

In his book, *The Power of Purpose: Creating Meaning in Your Life and Work,* Richard Leider writes, "With major change, we often confront, as seldom before, our own insecurities and self-doubts as we let go of the identity of the past and risk shaping our future. . . . Through purpose, we grow by becoming more honest with ourselves and more aware of our gifts that naturally give us joy."[3]

When we repress the need for change, it becomes an inner conflict. It doesn't go away. Psychologist Karen Horney states, "The more we face our own conflicts and seek out our own solutions, the more inner freedom and strength we will gain."[4] All of us desire inner freedom and strength. And the one way to receive this freedom is to face the truth about ourselves, which can be very disturbing. None of us wants to feel broken. But this is part of the human condition. The one thing we all have in common is the need to change something in our lives. And the way to accomplish change is by identifying with the developmental or environmental forces that are urging us to change.[5] This was the key for Kalma Graham. She identified with the health scare that was urging her to change. When she coupled the health scare with a great program at the Y, she succeeded.

The journey to freedom begins as we overcome low self-esteem and use the environmental and developmental pressures as modes of change. We begin to build a new relationship with ourselves—one day at a time.

The biblical book of Nehemiah tells the story of the rebuilding of the wall around Jerusalem after enemies had destroyed it. Nehemiah's first task was to survey the ruins. He walked around the broken-down wall and wept. Then he assembled a team of people and began to build. Almost immediately, interferences occurred. Their enemies were back to stop the rebuilding. They attacked the builders' self-worth. They yelled to the workers, "What they are building—if even a fox climbed up on it, he would break down their wall of stones!"[6] I'm sure laughter erupted among the enemies.

Enemies rose up against the project. There were those who tried to stop it. But Nehemiah set guards around the wall as the people worked, defeating the enemy's interference. And as we begin to consider the damage of our lives, seeing how we might rebuild, we will need people around us who can build a pocket of protection where we feel safe to become authentic. A place where we experience the freedom to discover our true selves, while surrounded by a healing community of people who extend grace and affirmation to us—the way the YMCA did for Kristy when she decided to lose 205 pounds and regain her health.

As we choose to trust and become authentic with others, we discover the power that comes from being part of a healing group. When I am in a group and I begin to tell the truth about myself, no one runs out the door. Instead, they all say, "Thank you. I'm so glad you are here!" This affirmation and acceptance in the face of my weakness is *grace*, the kind God gives me through other people.

May you find this group as a healing group. May you find the courage to become your true self. It's okay to use health scares, overdoses, DUIs, addictions, or whatever negatively controls your life as a catalyst for change. We've all reached that moment with you. And we all want to help you change.

REFLECTIONS

CHANGE USUALLY TAKES PLACE OUT OF DEVELOPMENTAL OR ENVIRONMENTAL FORCES THAT URGE US TO RETHINK OUR CONDITION.

• How has low self-esteem affected your life?

• Do you believe that self-worth is the foundation from which God transforms our lives?

• What do you really think about yourself?

HIDDEN PRISONS:
LIFE-CONTROLLING ISSUES

BREAKING THE CHAIN OF NEGATIVE THOUGHTS

I have memories invoked by the hum of lawnmowers in the distance. The smell of fresh-cut grass on sidewalks. The sound of a golf club making contact with a golf ball on the greens. All of these remind me of the golf course that loomed before us, as my father taught me how to golf. Those were wonderful times. I was nine or ten years old; I can't remember exactly. But I've never forgotten those summers or the golf swing that I developed under his tutelage. If you and I went golfing today, you would witness the same golf swing I developed back then. It's like riding a bike. You never forget.

Memory is a strange thing. Dr. Gerald May says, "Sadly, the brain never completely forgets what it has learned."[1] This is the human condition. It's like there is a chain that connects every thought we've ever had. Some links are massive. Other links we barely remember and can only recall with much effort. Then there are the corrosive links: those that try to destroy every good thought we've ever had, like a cancer, multiplying before we even begin to recognize them.

It would it be great if our minds could remember only pleasant things, but memory is no respecter of events. Memory interacts with the stimuli in our lives. This is why hearing a song may remind us of certain times in our lives. Memory involves the integration of thoughts past and present. And corrosive memories

SPIRIT

"Our Lord's confidence in God, and in what God's grace could do for anyone, was so perfect that he never despaired, never giving up hope for any person."

—OSWALD CHAMBERS,
MY UTMOST FOR
HIS HIGHEST

seem to stand out more than healthy ones. We also tend to associate negative thoughts of failure with our self-worth.

One thing we can ask ourselves is: *Am I more likely to remember positive memories, as well as negative ones?* If we can't balance the two, then we have disintegration. Disintegration happens when we allow negative thoughts to dominate our minds, and this causes us to be imbalanced. Then negative thoughts form one long chain of bad memories. This is the problem. Psychologist Arthur Freeman writes, "Remember that the more you repeat something, the more likely you are to keep it in the front of your mind. When you continue to review a mistake, a missed opportunity, or a wrong done to you in the past, you keep the memory fresh, the injury current, the loss immediate, and the pain fresh."[2]

Negative patterns of thinking that get repeated over and over again in our minds become deeply ingrained, causing us to approach life from learned patterns of helplessness, just as I approach golf today by the golf swings my father taught me almost forty-five years ago.

Psychologists believe that negative thoughts are a result of *rumination*, a close cousin to brooding. Martin Seligman writes, "The more you are inclined to ruminate, the more it arises. The more it arises, the more depressed you will be. Brooding, thinking about how bad things are, starts the sequence. Ruminators get this chain going all the time. Any reminder of the original threat causes them to run off the whole pessimism-rumination chain . . ."[3]

This chain of negative thoughts strung together by rumination needs to be broken. Once we fall into the trap, it is easy to link several bad occurrences together, such as linking the failure we experienced in 1986 with the one in 1991, and the one in 1999, followed by the one in 2005. These failures, when linked together, collectively create feelings of despair. We begin to believe that our whole life can be summed up by these events.

The way to break the rumination chain is by putting together a chain of good thoughts. This method is called *diversionary tactics*, in which you divert one set of thoughts by substituting another. Dr. Freeman says, "Diversionary tactics can be very effective in changing your mood and helping you to forget, because they interrupt the constant repetition of those thoughts that put you in a bad mood in the first place."[4]

Say you need to lose twenty pounds, and instead of thinking you can't do it, you start a new chain of thoughts by telling yourself, *I* can *change my weight.* Then add another thought: *I'm going to watch what I eat because eating plays a part in my being overweight.* Then the next thought could be, *I'm going to join the YMCA or some other health club and begin to work out.* All of these thoughts linked together begin to make a new chain. Scripture instructs us to "be changed within by a new way of thinking."[5]

The new way of thinking begins with a new thought. It's as simple and as hard as that. If we desire life without the present extra twenty pounds, then we have to think about what life would be like without the twenty pounds. The same way Joe Sobeck had to rethink never playing squash again.

Joe Sobeck was the best squash player at the Greenwich, Connecticut, YMCA. Some would say that he was *too* good at it, but who can blame them for not wanting to get demolished by him? Not many of us would play Tiger Woods in a round of golf if we were an average golfer. It might be fun to watch and learn from Tiger. But playing him week after week and losing would be humiliating. No one wants to lose on a continual basis. This was Joe Sobeck's problem. No one would play squash with him.

Frustrated by his lack of competition in squash and in an effort to continue playing sports with his friends at the Greenwich Y, Sobeck tried handball. But it was not to his liking. Handball hurt his hand. So, Sobeck was back where he started—a lonely squash player. This got Sobeck to thinking about how he might be able to utilize the handball court by combining the racquet from squash with the rubber ball from handball. Out of his dilemma, Joe Sobeck created a new sport—racquetball. He used his despondency as a catalyst for change. He had to think beyond not getting to play squash and rethink his entire situation. He did not "ruminate" on the negative, a term that first meant "chewing the cud." Sobeck combined two sports. He was proactive. We see this repeatedly in the history of the YMCA. Someone invents something great by rethinking the old grid.

Become aware of negative rumination. Try not to "chew the cud" of past failures. One negative thought can lead to another, until we assume that even the future is tainted. Then we begin to link negative thoughts into a chain of learned helplessness. We predict the future based upon our negative chain of thoughts. This is when we give up and believe the lie of negative rumination. We feel helpless.

A negative chain of thoughts breaks when we have our first positive thought. The Scriptures say, "[B]e changed within by a new way of thinking."[6] This means that our minds can overcome negative thoughts by thinking in a new way about our circumstances. Linking positive thoughts together, the way Joe Sobeck linked two sports, will create a diversionary chain that breaks the negative one. So, reevaluate every thought you have. Test each thought. Ask: "Is this thought leading to new thoughts or back to bondage?" Every positive thought will lead us further along the journey to freedom.

REFLECTIONS

NEGATIVE PATTERNS OF THINKING THAT GET REPEATED OVER AND OVER AGAIN IN OUR MINDS CAN BECOME DEEPLY INGRAINED BELIEFS.

- Are you a pessimistic or an optimistic person? Do your thoughts affect your behavior? Are you easily depressed? Do you have a feeling of hopelessness?

- Do you have the ingrained belief that your problem will never change? If so, why?

- Are you pessimistic or optimistic about your ability to change?

- Do your thoughts reflect your behavior?

OVERCOMING A STATE OF FEAR

Jerry Seinfeld once said that when at a funeral, most of us would prefer to be in the casket than the one delivering the eulogy. Most of us can relate, because surveys show that we fear public speaking more than death.

Numerous organizations today provide services to help conquer the fear of public speaking. One professional company advertises that they can cure the fear of public speaking in twenty-four hours. If that's true, then sign me up! But I'm afraid I won't get my money's worth. No seminar will help me be able to speak in public like Ronald Reagan.

Fear can take place in many arenas of life, not just with public speaking. In *Embracing Fear and Finding the Courage to Live Your Life,* Thom Rutledge writes, "Fear is our constant companion, our day-to-day nemesis, and our ultimate challenge. Fear fuels our negative and judgmental thoughts and our need to control things. Fear underlies guilt and shame and anger."[1] This is so true. If I were going to tackle my fear of public speaking, I'd join a Toastmasters club. They are the original "fear-busters" of public speaking. In October 1924, in the basement of the YMCA in Santa Ana, California, a group of men assembled by Dr. Ralph C. Smedley formed a club "to afford practice and training in the art of public speaking."[2]

The Toastmasters Club has helped men to overcome fear of public speaking for over eighty years, which lets us know that fear is here to stay, but also that it is vulnerable to our attacks. If we can overcome the fear of change, we have won 75 percent of the battle. Fear is that critical. The one phrase Christ used more than any other was "fear not." He knows that people change only when they feel safe. He knows fear is a black plague of the mind that holds us in bondage and keeps us from enjoying a lifetime of hope, health, and happiness. I know, because fear influences my own life and at times threatens my faith. It keeps me from loving people. It makes me feel hopeless when God promises so much to be hopeful about.

As human beings, there are four key fears with which we struggle: 1) fear of death, 2) fear of responsibility, 3) fear of isolation, and 4) fear of meaninglessness. Almost all of us wrestle with these fears at one time or another. Out of the four, the fears of isolation and meaninglessness may be the most difficult to bear.

Psychotherapist Dr. Irvin D. Yalom, who has provided forty years of oversight to group therapy sessions called "process groups," asked the participants in his groups to engage in a "top-secret" task. They were each instructed to write down one thing that they did not want the group to know about them. The most common secret in the group was a deep conviction of basic inadequacy—a feeling that they were incompetent in everything they did. The next frequent response was a deep sense of interpersonal alienation—that despite appearances, they were incapable of loving another person.[3]

We find this to be true in the people with whom we work at Restore Ministries. There is a deep-seated fear of inadequacy across the board. Most of them feel that they are not smart enough, good-looking enough, or skilled enough. They say, in essence, "If you really knew me, you would reject me. I'm unlovable." So, they go through life waiting on a feeling of absolute certainty. They want to be absolutely certain that no one will reject them before they take any kind of risk. They want to be absolutely certain that they will not fail when they change. They want to be absolutely certain that if they risk anything in life, they will beat the odds. But no one can be absolutely certain of these things. This is the reason most people never take risks.[4] They are waiting for

MIND

"We cannot escape fear. We can only transform it into a companion that accompanies us on our exciting adventures. . . Take a risk today— one small or bold stroke that will make you feel great once you have done it."

—SUSAN JEFFERS

something that no one will ever experience when it comes to change—absolution. Change is not waiting for us to become perfect. It's like the person who says they will go to church once they stop sinning. They will never attend if that is their criteria for attendance. Likewise, people who say they will change only when they can be absolutely certain they will not fail never do.

When someone stands up to give a speech, they are not absolutely sure the audience is going to receive them or the speech well. If we had 100-percent assurance of success, then there would be no need for Toastmasters! Speeches are a series of risks. We risk when we put our material together. Will it be interesting and informative? Does the audience need to hear about the subject on which we are speaking? Will the audience find us winsome? Are we able to deliver the message without obstructions in our voice or mannerisms that might take away from the message? Speeches are a series of risks. So is change. Nothing is absolute.

Bob Parsons, founder of *www.GoDaddy.com*, tells the story of three panelists who were slated to discuss a certain topic. When the first panelist stood, he was so nervous that he finally had to say, "I'm sorry, I cannot continue." Everyone felt terrible for the guy. But after the other two panelists had finished, the first panelist grabbed the microphone and said, "If you don't mind, I'd like to try to deliver my presentation now." Bob Parsons said that the audience was very attentive, and when he finished, they gave him a standing ovation.[5] I'm sure the guy didn't deliver a flawless speech. But he took a risk, and people everywhere admire those who have the guts to try again after failure. This is a good example of training versus trying.

I'm sure the panelist that first failed to give his speech found courage after he listened to the other two, perhaps because they didn't deliver perfect speeches, either. Maybe he realized that there *are* no perfect speeches. Maybe he recognized their flaws. Fear of public speaking is part of a greater fear—the fear of inadequacy.

If fear of inadequacy is the problem, then security is the cure. So, how do we begin to feel secure enough to risk? The psalmist says in the Bible, "I said, 'I am about to fall,' but, LORD, your love kept me safe."[6] Understanding God means that we realize that He is for us and not against us. Those who feel safe have a tendency to change more than those who fear.

It takes a vision and purpose for life to defeat fear. Much of what I believe can be summed up in a verse from the book of Jeremiah. It states: "'I know what I am planning for you,' says the LORD. 'I have good plans for you, not plans to hurt you. I will give you hope and a good future.'"[7] I vowed that with God's help, I would no longer live in bondage to fear. And the moment I began to trust God, I overcame fear. What other choice do we have, really? We can worry. We can feel inadequate. We can fear we will never be loved. I feared this for years. I was single for an extended period of time in my life. There were moments when I thought God had no plans left for my life. Then I met someone and recently remarried. What a feeling to know that God had a plan and a person for me all along. Maybe, at this moment, you need to exhale all of the fear and tension you feel. Now inhale the wondrous promise of God— that His plans for you are good. Draw new courage. We were meant to live in freedom. As the psalmist said, "I asked the LORD for help, and he answered me. He saved me from all that I feared."[8]

REFLECTIONS

**FEAR FUELS OUR DESTRUCTIVE RESPONSES TO LIFE AND
STEALS OUR FREEDOM TO EMBRACE OUR POTENTIAL.**

• How has fear influenced your desire to change?

• What are your inadequacies?

• Do you concentrate more on your inadequacies than your potential
for change?

DENIAL AND PROCRASTINATION

Dan woke up one day and decided to change. It was as simple and as hard as that. He stood five feet, eight inches tall, weighed 412 pounds, and had been in denial for a long time. Dan said when buying a new car, he didn't compare prices and styles or gas-mile efficiency. Instead, he bought the car that he could fit into. When he frequented restaurants, he asked for a table. Booths were too small, and sitting in chairs with armrests were like being gripped in a vise. He had to ask for seatbelt extensions when he traveled on planes, which stressed him out. He hated his life.

He even says, "When I weighed 412 pounds, I had started making a photo album for my daughters, because I didn't think I'd be around much longer."

Then Dan purchased a popular book on weight management and began to work out at a YMCA in Rhode Island, believing it was not just about diet. This time it was about a lifestyle change.[1] It was about the truth of his condition. It was about getting out of denial.

DENIAL OVER THE LONG HAUL

H. L. Mencken once said, "All men are frauds. The only difference between them is that some admit it. I myself deny it." Denial is the great enabler that keeps us from change. It teaches us to say, "I don't have a problem. I'm okay. I'm in control." It is a self-protective way of not looking at the truth about ourselves. From my experience in recovery and healing and the thousands of people with whom I have worked, I have seen that so many of us are in denial. We believe no problem exists—like Phil, who received multiple DUIs and kept going to jail, but denied his role in his troubles. Most blame bad luck or believe the police have somehow singled them out. When we start blaming everyone else for our problems, it's a good indicator that we may be deceiving ourselves.

Denial has been around a long time, and with it comes blame. Most people in denial want other people to change, and so they blame. Adam blamed Eve for his part in eating the forbidden fruit in the Garden of Eden. Cain killed his brother, and then whined when God confronted him. Cain said to God, "My punishment is more than I can bear. Today you are driving me from the land, and I will be hidden from your presence; I will be a restless wanderer on the earth, and whoever finds me will kill me" (Genesis 4:13–14 NIV). This may very well be the first pity-party in history. Cain killed his brother and then blamed God for the consequences, making God the bad guy.

Not only do we blame others, but we also hide from them. Laura had lived most of her life in isolation before coming to Restore Ministries. Her bedroom was her hideout. Every night and weekend, she huddled there in fear, because the task of maintaining her false self had become overwhelming. In this place of isolation, her addictions thrived, along with her insecurities, even though she thought she was protecting herself from rejection and pain. Through her own journey to freedom, she escaped the bondage of shame and isolation and is now living a life filled with hope. At Restore, she found a safe place to be honest and vulnerable, a place to take a risk to overcome her feelings of inadequacy. And this risk needed to take place in front of others who would accept her and point out falsehoods. Dr. Prochaska believes that so many people struggle to stay in their isolation because it feels safe there. You can't fail in isolation.[2] It leads to the erroneous belief that you can change later, which leads to the next enabler.

Procrastination is another tremendous enabler. Procrastination is another form of denial. It causes us to overlook our problems. Whereas denial is a rejection of the truth, procrastination accepts the truth but delays the action it takes to correct the problem, creating a habitual pattern. Most procrastinators live six months out. They think, *I'm going to do something about this, but let's just give it six more months to see what happens.* We procrastinate because we don't want to confront the truth about ourselves. We don't want to walk down that difficult path; we don't want to do the work; we don't want to endure the pain or the discomfort that usually comes with change.

Some overweight brides keep postponing their weddings because they can't get motivated to look their best. *Psychology Today* reports that college students who procrastinate have higher levels of drinking, smoking, insomnia, stomach problems, colds, and flu.[3] It all comes back to fear. We fear that what we think about ourselves is true, that we are inadequate to change.

<table><tr><td>SPIRIT

"I fear nothing. I am free."
—NIOS KAZANTZAKIS,
GREEK WRITER</td></tr></table>

THE PSALMIST'S WAY

To overcome denial and procrastination, we will need to stop looking for a sensational solution or for a perfect program of change, because the longer we procrastinate, the harder it will ultimately be to change.[4] Determination and willpower play a large role, but not the deciding role. God's power, along with our powerlessness over our problems, results in the outcome the psalmist experienced.

In Psalm 139, the psalmist opens his life to examination: "God, examine me and know my heart; test me and know my nervous thoughts. See if there is any bad thing in me. Lead me on the road to everlasting life" (vv. 23–24). He didn't deny or blame; he simply asked God to change him. It's a huge difference. If we can get this right, many things will change for us. Notice the psalmist's weakness as he called on God's strength.

The psalmist was humble. He said, "God, examine me and know my heart . . ."[5] He knew that without God, he was powerless to change. He knew

God could pinpoint his problem. So, he opened the pain of his life up to God. In essence, he trusted God.

The psalmist recognized his nervous thoughts. "Test me and know my nervous thoughts."[6] There is another side of denial and procrastination that many people miss. We fail to see how it influences our self-worth. Many of us who struggle with shame and low self-esteem tell ourselves, *This is all I am. This is all I will ever be. This is all I will ever know. Can't you see who I am? I am a failure.* I believe this is often more difficult than seeing the negatives of our behavior. M. Scott Peck once said that neurotics drive themselves crazy, while psychotics drive everyone else mad. The psalmist admitted his nervous thoughts. He decided it was time to stop blaming and denying.

The psalmist was willing to change. He said, "Lead me on the road to everlasting life."[7] All we bring to this journey is our willingness to be led. We need to be willing to open up and allow God and other people to help us change. When we pray, "God, lead me," He may use other people in our lives to help guide us. This is where community takes on a significant role in the process of change. One of the neat things about Dan's story is the way he started a new group at his YMCA. With help from the staff at the Y, he put together a weight-loss support group program and opened the doors to anyone interested in joining. He expected a small turnout, maybe ten to twenty people. But more than 100 attended that night, and over the course of the ten-week program, they lost a total of 916.5 pounds and 644 inches from their waists. The numbers are incredible!

The power of a group cannot be underestimated. Dan says, "I've gotten a lot of people at the end of each group coming to me and saying thank you. I'm not doing this. They're doing this. Everybody is taking care of themselves. Something that started as a very selfish journey has allowed me to give back to everyone else."

If we isolate ourselves, we will procrastinate, remain in denial, and miss the power of an examined life. Plato once said, "The life that is not examined is not worth living." Accountability is important as we begin to think about change. To move out of denial and procrastination, we need the help of God, His Spirit, and other people in a place where we can get the support, encouragement, love, and accountability that we need. We can't do this alone.

One of the most inspiring persons God brought into my life was a woman named Sheryl. She came into my life at a time when I was in despair. We would talk about life and the vision I wanted to see come to pass. She would always tell me, "I am for you, and I believe in you." She was one of the most incredibly pure, Spirit-filled, loving, godly persons that I've ever met. She was like Jesus in the flesh. I told her everything about me; all my depravity was exposed. And she would remind me of God's love. Sheryl showed me grace, the most powerful force in the universe, and it came in the form of a person telling me she knew where I came from, but she also knew where God could take me if I opened my life to Him. I'm sure this is probably what those in Dan's group felt—a freedom to change. This same journey to freedom is available to you.

REFLECTIONS

DENIAL IS THE GREAT ENABLER THAT KEEPS US FROM CHANGE. IT PREVENTS US FROM SEEING THE TRUTH IN OURSELVES.

• Are in you in denial about any aspects of your behavior?

• Do you isolate yourself from other people?

• Do you blame others for your problems?

_____

SILENCING THE INNER CRITIC

Warren Bennis once wrote about a promising junior executive at IBM who was involved in a risky venture for the company and ended up losing ten million dollars in the gamble. Later, he was called into the office of Tom Watson Sr., the founder and leader of IBM for forty years.

The junior executive, overwhelmed with guilt and fear, blurted out: "I guess you've called me in for my resignation. Here it is. I resign."

Watson replied, "You must be joking. I just invested ten million dollars educating you; I can't afford your resignation."

We can only imagine how the junior executive must have felt to be forgiven. But, like us, he probably struggled with forgiving himself. He had made a ten-million-dollar mistake!

Maybe you've made some mistakes in your career. Maybe you've let your spouse down again. Maybe you've promised more than you could deliver. Now you feel hopeless and foolish, and that small voice inside is cutting you, insulting you, abusing your self-worth. But that voice is a liar. God's investment in us is huge. He created us. He took the time to fashion us in our mothers' wombs. Then He sat at His desk and drew up blueprints for our lives. He knows there will be mistakes and detours. He knows humans aren't perfect, so why do we think we have to be?

MIND

"As we begin to pry ourselves loose from our old self-concepts, we find that our new, emerging self may enjoy all sorts of adventures."

—JULIA CAMERON,
THE ARTIST WAY

Inside each of us, there is an inner critic who reminds us of our frailty and faults. Some of the inner criticism stems from something in our past. As a child, we may have suffered verbal abuse. Then there are those of us that believe we have to be perfect. We believe we have to be the model parent and the role model for men and women everywhere. We believe that we have to win every contest in the boardroom. We make life hard on ourselves, and listening to our *inner critic* leads to despair and the loss of self-worth, which often leads to addiction and other risky behavior. We devalue ourselves and place ourselves in the discount bin. This is a clear sign that something is wrong inside of us; when nothing we do brings a sense of value, and we tend to believe that our life doesn't matter.

The inner critic stems from a sense of inferiority. We believe others perceive us as failures because we perceive ourselves as failures. We personify the inner critic, making it the spokesperson for the way the world sees us. It nags and deceives. No matter how we perform, it likes to tell us what we "should" have done, not allowing us to enjoy any success. It makes us feel deeply inadequate.

For me, overcoming the inner critic has been a lifetime struggle. No matter what I achieved athletically or professionally, I never thought it was enough. And this led to the performance trap and to my becoming an approval addict. I felt that I must win outside approval in order to feel good inwardly, which eventually split me into two sides—the defeated side and the side that kept up a false front, as if everything were perfect.

When you have negative beliefs about yourself—if you believe at your core that you are inadequate—then you will begin to pretend to be the person that you believe others want you to be. You will develop what we call a "false self" in order to cope with the reality of the issues you're dealing with versus the person you want others to believe you are. I've seen this pattern occur with men and their sexual addictions. They use fantasy to escape the inner critic. Somehow it feels safe to them. It's a way to love themselves when they feel that no one else will. Fantasy never makes judgments.

For many of us, abuse was a part of our childhood, whether it was active, passive, emotional, or sexual; whether it was sarcasm, parental over-control, or just plain negativity. I met someone in Restore whose mother had left her alone as a small child while she went out for extended periods of time. Her mother would leave behind junk food and videos to console her daughter. As an adult, this young woman struggled with self-worth and an eating disorder. Another person in Restore had had a dad who berated him and told him he was stupid: "You're lazy. You can't do anything right." Over time, he began to believe it. The voice became a hounding inner critic.

When we carry these kinds of negative messages inside of us from our childhood, we will struggle with inferiority. Eventually we begin to believe these negative messages. Then to silence the inner critic, we self-medicate with substances or activities of escape. No one can live long with the inner critic without falling into a pattern of risky behavior to silence it.

The inner critic uses comparison to devalue. The inner critic compares us to those who seemingly have the prestige and power we desire. Never does it compare us to those who have less. It makes us feel as if we are the only ones being deprived of the "good life." This causes us to feel devalued and to feel as if we are second-class citizens to those we view as successful.

ALWAYS SECOND-GUESS THE INNER CRITIC

Swimming and aquatics have long been associated with the YMCA, and over the years, tens of millions of people across the country have learned to swim at the YMCA. But this hasn't always been the case. In the early years, swimming suffered at the hands of its critics. Most viewed swimming as a distraction from legitimate physical development. Boys in San Francisco, for example, could not use the pool until after they had passed a proficiency test in gymnastics, as if swimming were mere child's play. Of course, those critics were wrong.

MIND

"Go confidently in the direction of your dreams! Live the life you've imagined."

—HENRY DAVID THOREAU

We should never devalue something until we understand its positives aspects. Always make conclusions about yourself and others by evaluating not only the negative comments, but also the positive ones.

It might work something like this: Say the inner critic points out a negative trait about yourself that makes you cringe. Instead of taking that negative trait and running with it, state something positive back to the inner critic. If it says, "You are a terrible mother. Look at how your children behave," then you must dispute its claim. Instead of believing the inner critic, focus on the good things you have done for your children. Being a soccer mom or taking your child and his or her friends to see a movie the previous week should count as something positive. Be careful not to disqualify the positives. By disputing with the inner critic, you will silence it.

Swimming at the YMCA needed someone to dispute the negative aspects and point out the positive ones. One of the developments that helped change the attitudes of the YMCA staff toward pools was the development of mass swim lessons in 1907 by George Corsan at the Detroit YMCA. Corsan taught swimming strokes on land, starting with the crawl stroke first as a confidence builder. He developed the ideas of the learn-to-swim campaign and used bronze buttons to reward swimming proficiency.

In 1932, there were more than a million swimmers a year at YMCA pools. In 1984, it was reported that YMCAs collectively were the largest operator of swimming pools in the world. All of this happened because someone became convinced that swimming could overcome its negatives. Corsan refused to disqualify the positive. He understood the value of swimming as an exercise.

Change takes place when we silence the inner critic. Positive change heals our souls and recaptures our hearts. It is essential to have people in our lives that can confirm and love us, holding us accountable, so we can begin to hear affirmations that drown out the voice of the inner critic.

Max Lucado has a beautiful children's book titled *You Are Special.* It is a story of a town of wooden characters, called Wemmicks, where performance decides self-worth. Some Wemmicks can jump tall boxes. Some know big words. Others can sing pretty songs. When they do something special, everyone gives them stickers shaped like stars. But those who seemingly have no talents and are chipped and rough along the edges receive gray dot stickers. If they fall or look stupid, everyone gives them dots. Among these dot-littered Wemmicks is Punchinello, who believes he deserves every dot he receives.

One day Punchinello meets a very different and kind Wemmick named Lucia, who has no dots or stars. She's just wooden. And when Punchinello asks her how to avoid receiving stickers from the other Wemmicks, she tells him to go visit Eli, the wood carver who made him.

When Eli meets Punchinello, he places Punchinello on his bench, looks over the dots, and says, "Looks like you've been given some bad marks."

"I've tried real hard."

"Oh, you don't have to defend yourself to me, child. I don't care what the other Wemmicks think . . . and you shouldn't, either . . . You are special!"

Punchinello says, "Me, special? Why? I can't walk fast. I can't jump. My paint is peeling. Why do I matter to you?"

Eli places his hands on Punchinello's shoulders and says, "Because you are mine. That's why you matter to me."

Every day, Punchinello visits with Eli and hears how special he is—and his dots start hitting the ground. Because Punchinello refuses to continue to believe what the other Wemmicks think about him, he is free from a life of gray dots.[1]

There is a God who values you because He made you and loves you just as you are, and the more you are open to hearing that fact each day, the more you will realize who you are. You will begin to accept that you are special because God made you, and this will silence the inner critic every time.

REFLECTIONS

THE INNER CRITIC STEMS FROM A SENSE OF INFERIORITY.

- Do you struggle with negative feelings about yourself?

- Do you vehemently criticize yourself?

- Do you compare yourself with others who seem more successful?

ADDICTIVE THINKING

Early pools at the YMCA posed a health threat to the swimmers. In addition to being small, the pools had no filters or circulation systems, so the water in the pools would eventually become filthy. Maintenance would then have to drain them and refill. But this "negative" was solved when Ray L. Rayburn, a founder of the Building Bureau of the YMCA (now Building and Furnishing Services), came up with the idea to use filtration systems to keep the water clean. It was a system of replacement. Water flowed into a filter and came out totally clean and different. It revolutionized swimming at the Y, because pools no longer posed a health threat.

Change is a program of replacement. As we begin to practice new self-dialogue and affirmations and visualize the new person we want to become, these new ways begin to take root and replace the old behaviors. It's like digging up a weed-laden garden. We uproot the old and make way for the new. We go in, plant new seeds, water them, and give them time to grow and establish roots. It takes time, patience, and a very vigilant effort.

Time is the maturing process. God needs time. We need time. Over the years, in working with people in recovery at Restore, we have seen every form of addiction. We have seen various life-controlling issues that are deeply entrenched in people's lives. These behaviors, moods, and thought patterns become a way of life. They rule people's lives and steal a lifetime of hope, health, and happiness.

The definition of *addiction* found in Gerald May's book, *Addictions and Grace,* is "any compulsive habitual behavior that limits the freedom of human desire."[1] Anything that puts us in bondage is a sick and sinful pattern, and addictions only contaminate our lives even more. Think of the pools before filtration systems were invented. The trapped water soon became dirty water, limiting the freedom of using the pool. People worried about the health problems associated with dirty pools. In addition, it was very difficult and time-consuming to drain the water and clean the pool, so, once again, the positives were trapped inside the negatives.

When trapped inside addictive behavior, we become a polluted pool. The dirty water taints everything. We approach life from this contamination. We corrupt our relationships with God and people. We bring them into this sinful pattern, this closed system of contamination.

The more effort we make to gain control, the stronger our addictions become and the weaker our resistance. What starts out as an effort to stay thin becomes an addiction to dieting or purging. What begins as an attempt to set things in order turns into obsessive-compulsive disorder. We use sex as a means to get love, but soon lose sight of the love because we are blinded by the sex. And just because we may not struggle with the so-called extreme addictions doesn't mean we're not addicted. Anything can become an addiction—work, gambling, fitness, overeating, alcohol, caffeine, cleanliness, approval. The more human effort we put into trying to control these urges, the stronger the impulse becomes. When we use addictions as a filtration system in an attempt to cleanse problems from our lives, they only make matters worse.

God says, "Come, let us talk about these things. Though your sins are like scarlet, they can be as white as snow. Though your sins are deep red, they can be white like wool."[2] God offers a different filtration system to cleanse our souls from sick and sinful patterns.

The first element in the new filtration system is an open relationship with God. He says, "Come, let us talk." It's an invitation. Notice that He doesn't say, "Go do thirty-eight things, then come back and let's talk." He says, in essence,

"Let's contemplate your life *as is* and discuss how I can help cleanse it."

It's true that we never defeat addictions on our own. God is the filtration system that will wash out the impurities. The way to detach our lives from addictions and attach them to this new filtration system is to realize that we can't cleanse ourselves. We are powerless against our addictions—permanently tainted and stained. We need something beyond our own human power. We need God's help.

> ## SPIRIT
>
> "Every blade of grass has its Angel that bends over it and whispers: Grow, grow."
> —The Talmud

The second element is decontamination. We become willing to allow God to cleanse us with His grace. We're ready to reach out and take the hand of hope. We understand that we have nowhere else to turn. This is what Jesus alluded to in the Sermon on the Mount, "Blessed are the poor in spirit" (Matt. 5:3 NIV). Blessed are those who understand that the worst poverty on earth can happen in our souls.

One day I was talking to a friend who was going through a tough bout of depression. His life was in turmoil. He was sitting there, talking and gazing around the room, when his eyes stopped. He had fixated on a list of the Beatitudes that I have hanging on my office wall, and he remarked, "I guess 'Blessed are the poor in spirit' means you're blessed when all you have to hope in is God." I think that is one of the the greatest definitions of what Jesus meant in that beatitude.

When we come to the end of ourselves and our self-sufficiency has failed, we arrive at a place of total defeat. When all I can do is throw up my hands and say, "I surrender. God, I need You," this is the beginning of real hope and the beginning of God's transformation of my life.

Dr. Gerald May says, "We will never really turn to God in loving openness as long as we are handling things well enough by ourselves. And it is precisely our most powerful addictions that cause us to defeat ourselves, that bring us to the rock bottom realization that we cannot finally master everything. Thus, although in one sense addiction is the enemy of grace, it can also be a power-ful channel for the flow of grace. Addiction can be, and often is, the thing that brings us to our knees."[3]

POWERLESSNESS IS ALL GOD NEEDS

In the movie *Castaway,* Tom Hanks stars as Chuck Noland, a workaholic FedEx efficiency expert, who knows what it means to control things. He con-trols his time, his career, his girlfriend, even his thoughts. But all of this changes when his plane crashes in the middle of the Pacific. Noland soon finds himself stranded alone on a remote desert island, unable to control any aspect of his life for five brutal years. After his rescue, he tells his friend about the time he tried to kill himself while stranded on the island.

"I was never going to get off that island. I was going to die there totally alone. The only choice I had—the only thing I could control—was when, and how, and where that was going to happen.

"So, I made a rope and I went up to the summit to hang myself. I had to test it, of course, so I used a log . . . and the weight of the log snapped the limb of the tree. I couldn't even kill myself the way I wanted to. Then a warm feeling came over me like a blanket when I realized that I had power over nothing."

Almost everyone will eventually reach a moment of clarity when they real-ize they can't control every aspect of their lives. Human strength is limited.

The true source of change happens when we admit we're powerless. We put our hope for change in God's power. "If anyone belongs to Christ, there is a new creation. The old things have gone; everything is made new!"[4] Become this new person.

REFLECTIONS

TIME IS A MATURING PROCESS. GOD NEEDS TIME, AND WE NEED TIME FOR THE PROCESS OF GROWTH TO TAKE PLACE IN OUR LIVES.

- Can you change without God?

- What in your life are you still trying to control that may actually be out of your control?

JOURNEY TO A LIFE OF PEACE

If you made a list of the things you wanted out of life, what items would you include? In your youth, you would have no doubt listed some obvious things—beauty, fame, riches, maybe a luxurious car. But as the years go by, you begin to understand more and more that most of these things might not become realities, and even if they do, you realize these things cannot satisfy.

The older we get, the more we realize that the greatest of all gifts in life is love, with a close second being peace of mind. The craving for inner peace and contentment seems to be universal. We all want a sense of poise, an inner life integrated with cheerfulness, and the ability to live in harmony with other people. We want freedom from disorder—freedom from distraction, freedom from any strife or dissension—a state of tranquility and quiet that implies a strong faith in the midst of struggles. We desire the peace that only Christ can give: "I leave you peace; my peace I give you. I do not give it to you as the world does. So don't let your hearts be troubled or afraid."[1]

Many of us live fear-based lives. One of the attributes of living in fear is that we're always in need, which causes us to live in a state of anxiety. We worry about our children, our jobs, our health, and then we worry about terrorism and all the other things that are out of our control. We can't control everything with absolute assurance. We just can't.

These mysteries of life can wake us at night and cause us to stare at the ceiling in a state of anxiety. They can make our chest hurt. They can put our stomach in knots. But the journey of peace begins when we realize we can't control everything. When we let go of the uncontrollable, we discover a state of peace that produces an inner life of serenity, a feeling of warmth and contentment the world can't offer.

The first barrier keeping us from experiencing peace is our need to control every aspect of our lives. In Day 11, we learned that the true source of change happens when we admit we're powerless. We have to make peace with our brokenness and our inability to make life a fairytale. Bad things happen in life—to good people. There are many things we can't control—so we need to learn to let go. Don't take life so seriously. Learn to let go of the uncontrollable.

The second barrier keeping us from peace is living out of a state of need rather than a state of faith. When we live in constant anxiety, we can't contemplate change.

CHANGE + ANXIETY = OVERLOAD

Before we can change, we must be at peace with our limited human strength. We must give up trying to conquer life and learn to contemplate the inner life, where strength comes from God. Focus on an inner life of serenity by accepting happiness. It makes room for gratitude. It allows for hope and faith to enter the equation.

We find this principle in the Lord's Prayer: "Give us this day our daily bread" (Matt. 6:11 NKJV). Faith must be daily. Our needs are met daily. Instead of obsessing over the future, we need to focus on today. When we take the focus away from ourselves, we will experience real peace—the greatest gift of freedom. It's no longer about human relationships that we believe will make us happy or how much money we need in order to be content. It's the realization that choice is at the heart of peace. Freedom is understanding that our happiness is a choice. The one who chooses peace is peaceful. The mind that chooses contentment is content.

The third barrier keeping us from peace is unforgiveness. In recovery, the phrase is often recited: "Do I want to be right, or do I want to be at peace?" There's a lot of truth in this phrase. I know people who are in bondage to unforgiveness. They can't seem to see that most of the time their unforgiveness only hurts them. It does nothing to the perpetrator. This is why making amends is an important step.

MAKING AMENDS

Mary came to Restore alone and frightened, seeking peace with herself and with those closest to her after being diagnosed with a very aggressive form of breast cancer. Over the years, Mary had become estranged from her grown children. Now she felt the need to make amends as she went through steps eight and nine of our twelve-step program. God healed her heart and renewed her relationship with her children as she made amends.

This is something all of us will eventually do if we decide to enter a twelve-step program. But whether or not you actually go through the program, you will need to deal with unforgiveness. Unforgiveness can build up over the years and destroy valuable time we might be able to spend with loved ones. As Mary realized, sadly almost too late, life is far too short to squabble with those whom we should love.

Forgiveness will set you free. A good indicator of where the relationship is at is how you feel at the mention of the other person's name. Do you get tense? Do you feel resentment? It could be unforgiveness coming to the surface. Although there's no surefire way to know when you've made complete amends, usually truth will set you free from these feelings.

Mary met a group of loving people at Restore who helped her through the final stages of her life. She wasn't healed physically, but her heart was healed before her death, and her pursuit of making amends also healed many other people in the group. It was grace that produced peace. It was *universality.*

If you are facing death, money and status don't matter, but peace certainly does. We can miss this. Some never get it. Mary did. So, the point we should contemplate is, what would be our response if, like Mary, we only had six months to live? Would we seek peace or money?

I want to come to the end of my life in a peaceful state of tranquility, knowing I'm at peace with God and with those whom I love. I desire an inner life that is free of resentment and anger—free of obsession—free of anxiety. Peace is what God intended for each of us.

One of the most beloved hymns ever written is "It Is Well with My Soul." It is a beautiful hymn with powerful words, and I feel so much peace whenever I sing it. The man who wrote it lost four of his daughters when the ship they were aboard collided with another ship. His wife survived and sent him the now famous telegram, "Saved alone." The hymn was birthed out of his grief.

This background allows you to see the words of the hymn with new eyes. You hear the music with different ears. It is hard to understand how a man could write such a hymn when facing such sadness—unless you know the Author of all peace, the One who gives what the Bible calls "the peace of God, which passeth all understanding."[2] This peace means that we don't have to have life all figured out. It leaves the uncontrollable and unanswerable questions to Him, because sometimes "why" is a mystery.

Several weeks later, as the man's own ship passed near the spot where his daughters had perished, he was inspired to write these words:

When peace, like a river, attendeth my way,
When sorrows like sea billows roll;
Whatever my lot, Thou has taught me to say,
It is well, it is well, with my soul.

The journey of peace begins when we stop trying to conquer the world with our own strength and begin to build an inner life that lives beyond the circumstances and for the peace of God. A life of hope, health, and happiness begins and ends with peace.

REFLECTIONS:

MANY OF US LIVE FEAR-BASED LIVES.

ONE OF THE ATTRIBUTES OF LIVING IN FEAR IS THAT WE'RE ALWAYS IN NEED, WHICH CREATES A STATE OF ANXIETY.

• If you made a list of what you want out of life, what items would you list?

• If you made a list of what you need in life, what items would you list?

• Could you live—and be happy—without your wants?

CREATING CHANGE

UNIVERSALITY: YOU'RE NOT ALONE

Universality: You're not alone. I learned this phrase from a therapist friend of mine. We were talking about community and what makes a group a powerful tool for healing, and this is when he used this phrase. He said that a group provides a sense of *universality*, which simply means "we're not alone." Others have the same or similar issues as we do. We struggle together. You realize you're not alone.

In the movie *Warm Springs*, there is an early scene in the beginning of Roosevelt's career in politics when he is diagnosed with polio, and the doctor tells his wife and his mother that his life will never be the same. He will have to deal with the life-changing difficulties of paralysis. This diagnosis pushes FDR into a spiral of despair, and he even struggles with wanting to simply give up on his life. Then he hears about a place in Georgia with hot springs where people with polio were going for therapy. His healing begins the moment he arrives. He understands the power of *universality*. He finally sees that others are dealing with the same issues that he has. This place becomes a setting of transformation and healing for FDR. He is forever grateful. He discovers his life again, and experiences the beginning of hope and healing around other people who are struggling with similar trials. Their strength and courage inspire him. Their honesty and tears move him. Their weakness causes him to risk vulnerability.

SPIRIT

"The events in our lives happen in a sequence in time but in their significance to ourselves they find their own order . . . the continuous thread of revelation."

—EUDORA WELTY

Seeing others struggle with like problems draws us out of isolation and into a place of safety. In the company of those similar to us, we can discover a place of healing. One of the greatest truths about growth and healing is that "I can't do it alone." I need others. I need their support. I need their encouragement. I need their love. I need their accountability. Most people will not abandon us or reject us if we become honest and confess our struggles. Most will meet us in our pain and comfort us.

Working with people in the process of change over the years, I've witnessed the greatest breakthroughs when—after first starting the program with feelings of shame and isolation—people start opening up and become vulnerable. They begin to speak openly about their struggles. It's like a monstrous burden is lifted off their souls. They no longer feel alone.

When we come out of isolation and begin to listen to others, we hear stories of struggle that we thought belonged to us exclusively. It's so freeing to hear that other people struggle, too. We realize we aren't alone—and that's universality. We begin to open up and feel hope. We feel a sense of companionship and community with others. We're in this together. We all want the same thing—to change and get better.

One of the greatest examples of the truth of universality is what I've seen over the past ten years working with men who struggle with sex addictions or pornography. It's a very shameful issue, very secretive. The nature of it is to hide in fantasy. It keeps them isolated and is so damaging to their self-esteem and sense of dignity. But when these men take the first step and enter a group with other men who have a similar struggle, many will break down and cry when they realize they are not alone. They feel shameful and remorseful. But they also sense hope, like Steve did.

Steve lost his job because of a sexual liaison with a married coworker. His wife separated from him and took the children. He had been very involved in his church and in the community where he lived, and because of his actions, he felt deep shame. However, he needed genuine help and healing. He knew this. But he was afraid. He didn't know where to turn until someone mentioned Restore, and he joined a small group of men with the same struggles.

With tears in his eyes, he said, "I didn't think I could ever face this. I was so ashamed and sure that no one had fallen to this depth, especially no one in my position. But hearing all of you guys talk about your struggles made me realize that I'm not alone. There is hope for me. I can be in this kind of group. I can heal here."

Universality is always better. It creates one of the greatest dynamics in healing—a place of safety and compassion. When I come out of isolation and connect with a community of people who have struggled the same way I have, who have felt the same things I have felt, and who want the same things I want, this is the journey to freedom. This is grace. It's the meaning behind the proverb, "If you hide your sins, you will not succeed. If you confess and reject them, you will receive mercy."[1] Mercy is what we find in universality. We can't make it alone. We need relationships.

Universality is also the beginning of forgiving ourselves. Healing takes place as we extend to ourselves the compassion of forgiveness, which can be difficult. Sometimes we want to keep punishing ourselves. We beat ourselves up. But this can make us hopeless, bitter, and even more isolated.

We need to deal with our problems first by becoming aware of them, and then by moving to a level of self-forgiveness.

Many of us are shame-stricken. Our addictions and low self-worth have caused us to believe that God doesn't love us—couldn't possibly love us—because of the things we've done. But somehow we believe He loves everyone else, because there is no one as bad as we are, no one who has disappointed God as much as we have. When we come into a group and hear other people talking

> # MIND
>
> "Self-esteem is about trusting your ability to make appropriate choices and cope effectively with adversity."
> —DR. NATHANIAL BRANDEN

about their doubts, about how they feel God doesn't love them, that in and of itself is healing. We need to know that we are not the only ones feeling this way.

There's a story about a bum who died in Bellevue Hospital after stumbling to a washbasin in his squalid room in the Bowery. He was trying to shave, but slipped and hit his head. Someone discovered him lying in a heap, naked, and bleeding from a deep gash in his throat, semiconscious. Someone called a doctor, who closed the wound on the spot using black sewing thread, while the bum begged for a drink. Someone handed him a bottle of rum to calm his nerves. They dumped him in a paddy wagon, and then dropped him off at Bellevue Hospital where he languished. He did not eat for three days. He died an unknown bum.

A friend who sought him out was directed to the local morgue where the man lay among dozens of other nameless corpses with tags on their toes. The friend identified him, and when he scraped together the man's belongings, he found a ragged, dirty coat with thirty-eight cents in one pocket and a scrap of paper in the other—all his earthly goods. The scrap of paper had five words written on it, "Dear friends and gentle hearts." *Almost like the words of a song*, he thought. But why in the world would a forgotten drunk carry around a line of lyrics?

Maybe the derelict with the body of a bum still had the heart of a genius. For once upon a time, long before his tragic death at age thirty-eight, he penned songs that blessed the whole world, like *Camptown Races, Oh! Susanna!,* and *My Kentucky Home.* In all, he had written over two hundred songs that have become deeply rooted in American heritage. He was Stephen Foster, about whom no one seemed to care except one lone friend.[2] What if Stephen had been in a group, a loving and caring group, and understood the concept of universality? Would things have turned out differently? Maybe he longed for a group where he could say, "Dear friends and gentle hearts." Maybe that was the message on the small piece of paper. We will never know.

We all need a place of safety where we can discover healing. Don't stop until you find *universality.* You're not alone.

REFLECTIONS

UNIVERSALITY MEANS "WE'RE NOT ALONE."

- Do you believe you can accomplish the change you desire on your own?

- Do you have a small group of people with whom you can share your struggles?

- Can you forgive yourself for past failures?

ICEBERGS: HITTING OUR PROBLEMS HEAD-ON

Researchers have discovered that most people make efforts to change around their thirty-ninth or fortieth birthday.[1] There must be something about that age. Maybe it's a mental halfway point for most of us. Whatever the case, it's true. It's as if a bell goes off in our minds, and we jump into action. We decide to face down our problems. Confront them head-on. We schedule workout time at the gym because we don't like what we see in the mirror. We get serious about change.

This happened to Melvin. He turned forty and decided he needed to tackle his problems head-on. Melvin weighed around 600 pounds. He had fallen into a serious depression and took disability. He lost his house and spent over four months in a nursing home due to complications from his obesity—pneumonia, a collapsed lung, failed kidneys. He was growing closer and closer to the same fate as his obese mother, who had a stroke at the age of forty-three. He knew that if he didn't do something soon, he was going to wind up in the same situation, spending the rest of his life in a nursing home alone before an eventual early death. He knew that was not God's will for his life, so he promised God that he would change, that he would begin to take care of his body.

Inspired by the *Today Show*'s weatherman Al Roker's experience with gastric bypass surgery, Melvin realized he wasn't alone in his struggle with weight, and he, too, made the decision to have gastric-bypass surgery.[2] After the surgery, Melvin changed his eating habits and began to be hopeful again. He started working out at the YMCA—water aerobics, weightlifting, and cardiovascular exercise six days a week. He also joined Restore Ministries because he realized he needed emotional and spiritual healing as much as he needed physical healing.

Melvin had to deal with the issues that controlled his life. Through the Restore process, he discovered his eating was emotional. It was just a symptom of what was going on in his life. Beneath the surface were emotional issues that had led to his problem of obesity.

Think of the iceberg that sank the Titanic. If you look at an iceberg, you only see the small portion of ice that is above the surface of the water. The vast majority of the iceberg is underneath the water. In an effort to avoid a head-on collision with the iceberg, the Titanic turned, sideswiping the iceberg beneath the surface and ripping open the hull. Some believe that if the *Titanic* had hit the iceberg head-on, there would have been tremendous damage, but the ship might not have sunk.

We have to deal with our problems head-on. Every problem has the possibility to sink us if we try to sidestep it rather than hit it head-on. Beneath the surface of our problems usually looms a greater threat. Drinking, overeating, violent anger, sex addictions, thrill seeking—all of these could be symptoms of something deeper within us. We may wrestle with deep feelings of insecurity and low self-esteem, so we drink to medicate ourselves. It takes the edge of the pain away. It makes us feel stronger and more courageous. Then before we know it, we have a drinking problem. Just like the iceberg that sank the

> # MIND
>
> "Self-esteem is indispensable to mental health; without it our resilience in the face of life's problems was diminished . . . the negatives had more power over us than positives. The world was a frightening place."
> —DR. NATHANIAL BRANDEN

Titanic, if we don't deal with our underlying, deeply rooted issues, more—and worse—trouble will be ahead for us.

Avoiding problems will not do you any good. Tackle them. Expose them. Dealing with deep underlying issues is a necessary step in the process of change.

MY PERSONAL ICEBERG

Low self-esteem and insecurity have plagued me throughout my life. But I never wanted to deal with those issues. I manipulated my way around them. I avoided. I procrastinated. I ran from confrontation. Dealing with my defects and deep feelings of inadequacy was not (and is still not) pleasant. It made me feel broken. I tried to cope by medicating myself, but I soon discovered the things I ran to had begun to control my life. My methods of avoidance never set me free.

Twenty-one months after Melvin began to tackle his problems, he had lost 324 pounds. He went from being in a wheelchair to a walker, then to a cane, before finally walking on his own. Now he is off disability and works for the YMCA Restore Ministries. His quality of life has completely changed. He has been transformed. Melvin met his problems head-on and changed his life.

Long ago, mapmakers sketched dragons on maps as a sign to sailors that they would be entering unknown territory at their own risk. Some sailors would not sail into these unknown waters. Others saw the dragons as a sign of opportunity, as a possibility to discover new territory.[3] Each of us has mental and emotional maps with dragons designating certain areas of our lives. We are not sure what's there. We are afraid to venture out, afraid to look beneath the surface of the dragon. But dragons need to be slain. Icebergs need to be hit head-on.

New life is waiting. Be willing to take constructive steps toward meeting your challenges head-on. Deal with them—grow through them—and continue your journey toward a lifetime of hope, health, and happiness. This is what God wants for you.

REFLECTIONS

**EVERY PROBLEM HAS THE POSSIBILITY TO SINK US IF
WE TRY TO SIDESTEP IT AND NOT HIT IT HEAD-ON.**

- Do you believe your challenges in life can strengthen you and lead you to growth?

- Do you have any challenges in life you need to work through that you have been avoiding?

THE MOTIVATION OF CHANGE

Robert Roberts was a burned-out circus performer. The Big Top no longer thrilled him. He was tired of the spectacular stunts. Tired of the difficult traveling. Tired of all of the same faces, all out for a good time at the show. The thrill was gone in his spirit, mind, and body, and he walked away from it all. But he wanted to continue to stay in shape. So, in 1881, Roberts—while on staff at the Boston YMCA—inaugurated a system of exercise he termed *bodybuilding work*. He believed rigorous repetition of weightlifting could build up the body. But Roberts had no dumbbells, so he used leftover Civil War cannonballs. The workout was a success, but the young men in the YMCA found it boring. They longed for team sports, and soon Naismith invented basketball to help keep them involved.

Today bodybuilding, weightlifting, and other individual exercises have become popular in our culture. But most people have a hard time getting motivated to work out. Our mind will play tricks on us. Deceive us. Dissuade us. Keep us in the recliner. It is amazing the excuses we come up with to avoid exercise. Sometimes we lack motivation. Some of us are intrinsically motivated—Type-As, go-getters, self-starters. Others get motivated when it is quitting time at their jobs or when the doctor gives an ultimatum. Others struggle with a low-grade depression that exercise could help alleviate. Then there are those who refuse to work out altogether.

Personally, I've struggled with three bouts of low-grade depression in my lifetime. Once when I was in college, once in my twenties, and once in my late thirties. I don't think I really knew at the time what was happening. I just knew I was sad and confused. But those dark days of the soul taught me a great lesson. During the bout of depression that occurred in my thirties, I was working at the YMCA—early in my career. I searched endlessly for relief, and what I discovered that did more good than anything was an early-morning run. This always made me feel better. To this day, it still does.

I had no appetite and learned that not eating fed right into the hands of a deeper depression. Six, seven, eight hours with no food lowers serotonin levels, which actually enhances depression. If I ate well—in moderate amounts—every three to four hours, it helped to steady my mood. In the afternoon, I would either lift weights at the YMCA or swim. Both seemed to give me a sense of strength.

When I go for an hour-long hike on the trails at Radnor Lake State Park, near my home, my mind is free to listen to the sounds of the breeze through the leaves—the birds singing, the feeling of my feet on the earth, the sensation of the wind against my skin. Sometimes as I hike near the end of the day, the sky changes into beautiful reds and shades of purple. As I come to the peak of a hill, I occasionally see a turtle, a chipmunk, or a deer, or I hear the sound of an owl. I'm a young boy again. The changes in nature awaken a sense of change in me. Peace replaces the frantic feelings of being overwhelmed by the responsibilities of work and life. I need this refuge. I need this restoration. My heart is beating, my lungs are breathing in oxygen. Energy is being spent. The machine that is my body is being tuned and strengthened.

Exercise creates relaxation of the mind and body. There is a reconnection with God when we use our physical bodies in the ways they were meant to be used. There comes a sense that we are part of something bigger. We awaken

> **BODY**
>
> "Muscle growth in people ranging from sixty to ninety six years old was as great as could be expected in young people doing the same amount of exercise."
>
> —George Leonard and Michael Murphy, *The Life We Are Given*

89

to the profound sense of wonder of the miracle of life, of our bodies, our minds, our spirits.

As I exercise, I include my spirit by thinking of certain psalms I've memorized that always strengthen me. As I jog or lift weights, I put a Scripture verse on an index card in front of me and repeat the passage until I have it memorized. And as I'm growing spiritually, there's a change in my mental outlook. Optimism replaces pessimism. I'm changing and being transformed. When I feel my muscles responding to my workouts, I know that I am refilling my tank with energy. I think of my body as a gas tank that needs refueling. I'm responding to all three areas—spirit, mind, and body—that need a sense of balance. Real and lasting change comes through these three areas. Everything in the YMCA's mission confirms this. It's a place where we can mend our lives spiritually, mentally, and physically.

During my times of depression, I also found a wonderful therapist and some close friends to whom I would talk every day. They would just listen as I would process the deep wounds and sort through the darkness that had settled in my soul. They didn't try to fix me. They would just listen, and that taught me so much. It has even enhanced the work I do now at Restore.

In almost twenty years of working with people in the process of change at the YMCA and Restore, I have discovered these things to be true. We are whole beings, comprised of a spirit, mind, and body, and so are those around us. The spirit that discovers fulfillment in God is free of anxiety, the mind at peace with Him never needs to worry, the body vigorous with exercise is healthy, and all three together make up a short but full description of a lifetime of hope, health, and happiness.

REFLECTIONS

EXERCISE IS A WONDERFUL WAY TO INCREASE OUR SENSE OF WELL-BEING AND OUR SELF-ESTEEM, AND ALSO HELPS TO REDUCE STRESS IN OUR LIVES.

- What physical activities do you like to do?

- Are you physically active, and do you feel good about your health?

DO IT NOW: LIVING THE DASH

Agroup of business professors once decided to conduct a study with a group of monkeys. What follows is a vivid story of the effects of failure. The professors placed four monkeys in a room with a tall pole in the center. Suspended at the top of the pole was a bunch of bananas. One of the hungry monkeys started climbing the pole to get something to eat, but just as he reached out to grab a banana, the experimenters blasted him with cold water. Squealing, the monkey scampered down the pole and abandoned his attempt to feed himself. Each monkey made a similar attempt and was drenched with cold water. After attempting a few more times, they finally gave up.

The researchers then removed one of the monkeys from the room and replaced him with a new monkey. As the newcomer began to climb the pole to get the bananas, the other three monkeys, who'd tried but failed, grabbed him and pulled him down to the ground. It was a brave act of rescue. They'd tried. They'd failed. They'd felt the cold water in their faces. So, after the new monkey tried to climb the pole several times and was dragged down by the others, he, too, gave up and never attempted to climb the pole again.

The researchers continued to replace the original monkeys, one by one, and each time a new monkey attempted to get the bananas, the other monkeys would again drag him down before he could reach the fruit. In time, the room contained only new monkeys who never attempted to climb the pole for bananas, even though they themselves had never received a cold shower.

Our lives can easily mirror this experiment. We give up on our dreams after a few failed attempts. We stop looking up, but we really don't know why. The urgency of life becomes a lull. We sleep. We stop dreaming. We begin to medicate. But it never works, and this is our only journey. We only get one shot at life, and we must live it to the fullest.

> ## SPIRIT
>
> "The tragedy of man is what dies inside himself while he still lives."
>
> —ALBERT SCHWEITZER

THE DASH

If you look in the obituaries or at a tombstone, you will see the year the deceased was born and the year he or she died. In between those dates is a dash—representing all the years between birth and death. If I died today, my dash would be between the years 1954 and 2005. But I haven't died yet, so my dash is not complete. But it's possible to lose the urgency of the dash. As some say, "In life there are no dress rehearsals." This is our only journey, but we must begin to believe once again that the pole is worth climbing. The itsy-bitsy spider kept climbing the waterspout because it believed the sun would shine again, no matter how many times the blast of water washed it out. So, we have to believe again—believe that the dash is worth living.

However, the dash requires effort. It takes energy to climb the pole with three other monkeys pulling at our heels.

Most accomplishments come through tremendous perseverance. We all face the noonday demon: the drudgery of our jobs. Our drab existence. The meager pay. The Bible says that life is like running a race. There's the start, the middle, the end. The final lap is the hardest. The middle is where we spend the bulk of life—the dash is where we truly live.

None of us knows when the dash will end. The mortician will tack on that final date. Life will end. So, there is no better time for change than now. Mark Twain once said, "Never put off until tomorrow what you can do the day after

BODY

"One of the best things to do when you are revved up is to move your body. Exercise helps deplete the stress homones that are circulating through your body so that you can calm down faster."
—JULIAN WHITAKER, M.D., AND CAROLE COLEMAN, *SHED 10 YEARS IN 10 WEEKS*

tomorrow." We all think like this sometimes, don't we? We say, "I will quit drinking tomorrow," "I'm going to lose ten pounds starting tomorrow," "I'm going to start exercising tomorrow," or "I'm going to finally get a job I enjoy tomorrow." But it seldom ever happens, does it?

We need to maintain our vision. One of the great tragedies of life is to be held back by someone else's dash. In a way, this is what the monkeys were doing. They gave up because someone else's dash went wrong. They believed a lie.

Jack Welch, longtime CEO of General Electric, once said, "Control your destiny or someone else will!" There's a lot of truth in this. A different proverb says that borrowers are servants to lenders.[1] Debt can enslave us. We can amass more and more material possessions while we worry about them at the same pace. But the life of freedom sets its own course. We run our own race like Irwin Jaskulski. Jaskulski was born on September 24, 1902, in the Ukraine. He was too young to serve in World War I, but the war affected him, anyway. He had little to eat. He weighed only 100 pounds at age eighteen. "So, I decided something had to be done," he said. He set out to change. He began a lifetime regimen of calisthenics—eight pull-ups, thirty squats, and fifty sit-ups every other day. He rock-climbed, swam, kayaked, and ice-skated. He hiked the Austrian and Swiss Alps.

Later, at the age of ninety-four, he decided to enter a 100-meter dash in the 1997 Aloha State games. It was his first race since his early twenties. Regardless, he entered the race in his age group, set a record at the time, and won. He said in a jubilant burst, "I came, I saw, I won!" He ran it in 25.73 seconds. But the World Association of Veteran Athletes refused to accept his record. They would not recognize the time, saying that the officials and timing systems were not certified. Slowly they began to certify the officials, as

Jaskulski started training to improve. Two years later at the age of ninety-six, he tried again. With determination, he crossed the finish line in 24.01 seconds. He'd cut more than fourteen seconds from the record set in 1997 by Kazuhiko Tsutsumi. All of this at age ninety-six! As the buzz about his impressive accomplishments escalated, Jaskulski was invited by both David Letterman and Jay Leno to appear on their shows. He told them, "I run for my pleasure, health, and satisfaction, not publicity." Jaskulski was a man running a great race, and running at his own velocity.

Every day people of all ages come to the YMCA to reach the goal of improving their spirits, minds, and bodies. Each time I see a young child or a senior citizen walk through the door, I remember that it's never too early to start, and it's never too late to change. This encourages me, because when we stop growing, we stop living.

Some of us may feel stuck in our lives. We may believe that change is impossible. But nothing is impossible with God. The book of Jeremiah says, "I am the LORD, the God of every person on the earth. Nothing is impossible for me."[2] God has a vision for us, a dream for our lives. He knows the plans He has for us, plans for a hope and a future.[3] He wants to use our lives for His purposes. Either we will answer His call, or we will sit back and let our spirits die within us while we miss the most incredible gift—the gift of the dash. With God's help, we can overcome anything, and we can move forward and achieve great things with our dash.

Start living your dash today! Now is the right time and this is the right place, because the dash will eventually end.

REFLECTIONS

MOST ACCOMPLISHMENTS COME THROUGH TREMENDOUS PERSEVERANCE.

- Are you living your "dash"?

- Do you give up on your dreams after a few failed attempts?

- Are you procrastinating about change?

DISCARDING OLD BAGGAGE

Harland was a failure—the embodiment of discouragement and disappointment. He dropped out of school at fourteen and tried odd jobs. Became a farmhand and hated it. Tried being a streetcar conductor and hated that. At sixteen, he lied about his age and joined the Army—hated that, too. When his one-year enlistment was up, he headed for Alabama, tried blacksmithing, and failed. Then he became a railroad locomotive fireman with the Southern Railroad. He loved this job and wanted to be a railroad man for life. At age eighteen, he married. He had it all: a beautiful wife and a great job. Then failure struck again. The railroad fired him. When he arrived home that day, his wife announced she was pregnant. It seemed to Harland that he could not catch a break. Then one day while he was out job hunting, his young wife gave away all of their possessions and went home to her parents. He felt like a loser and became extremely depressed.

How could an eighteen year old have so much baggage so early in life? If this were all the failure he'd face in one lifetime, we would call it a "time of training." But Harland kept losing jobs for various reasons. Then, late in life, he settled into being a "chief cook and bottle washer" at a restaurant in Corbin, Kentucky. He did fine at this job until the new highway bypassed the restaurant and killed the business, and Harland lost what seemed to be his last job. He retired. A lifetime of hope, health, and happiness had evaded him. He had nothing.

BODY

"The sovereign invigorator of the body is exercise, and of all the exercises walking is the best."

—THOMAS JEFFERSON

Then the postman brought his first Social Security check. That day, something within Harland finally exploded. He did not want the government feeling sorry for him, and he got so angry that he took that $105 check and started a new business. At the age of eighty-six, he finally became a success. The man who had seemed destined for failure overturned his destiny and got a new lease on happiness, because Harland Sanders—"Colonel Sanders"—started a new business with his first Social Security check. That business was Kentucky Fried Chicken.[1]

You never know what's around the corner. One set of circumstances can set into motion a domino effect of great things in your life. But there will be failures, disappointments, setbacks, taxes, health complications, wayward children, and other problems. Life has its baggage—those things that weigh us down and keep us stuck in a disappointing life.

Once we've decided to enter the process of change, our baggage will have to be discarded. Old habits of overeating and not exercising, thrill-seeking, holding grudges, addictions, all of these old habits—and many like them—will have to be discarded. We must let go of these things because any baggage on the journey to freedom will weigh us down, discourage us, and keep us in bondage.

BATTLE IN THE TRENCHES

In the book of 1 Kings in the Bible, a pay-per-view-like battle took place between Elijah and the prophets of Baal at a place called Mt. Carmel. It was a real "battle in the trenches." Elijah had challenged the prophets of Baal to build an altar of wood and call out to Baal, their god of the sun, to send down fire to light the altar. They accepted the challenge, built the altar, and called on Baal. From early morning until noon, they called on their god. Nothing happened. Out of desperation, they jumped up and down and cried out. Nothing.

According to their customs, they cut themselves until their blood gushed—but still no fire. Nothing. The wood remained dry.

Next, it was Elijah's turn to build an altar and call upon God to light it. Elijah was so sure that God would answer, he made a big show of it all. He had a trench dug around the altar, and instructed his men to pour four pitchers of water on the wood. Then, as if that weren't enough, he had them do it a second time, and then a third time. And to send it over the top, he had them fill the trench with water, as well. When the event reached its climactic height, Elijah let out a deep roar, crying, "Answer me, O LORD!" The fire of the LORD fell down, consumed the altar, and licked up the water in the trenches. The people immediately hit their knees in worship, crying out, "The LORD, He is God."

> SPIRIT
>
> "One does not dis-cover new lands with-out consenting to lose sight of the shore for a very long time."
> —ANDRÉ GIDE

Elijah had experienced a miraculous resolution, and you would think he would've felt invincible at that moment. But when Queen Jezebel heard that Elijah had not only defeated the prophets of the god she worshiped, but killed them, as well, she put a bounty on his head. She wanted to kill him. And the man who had just defeated the prophets of Baal ran away in shivering fear. He ran for Beersheba, the southern limit of the land, and then walked another full day into the wilderness. He found a shade tree, plopped down, and said, "That's it. Take my life, LORD. I can't live like this any longer." One minute Elijah was on top of the mountain, and soon after he became so discouraged that he wanted to die.[2]

The journey to freedom is not a baggage-free one. New obstacles will pres-ent themselves, and old wounds may resurface. They may even make us run for a shade tree where we just want to give up and die. Beginning the process of change with these obstacles and expectations in mind will help us under-stand that this journey is a progression, not a destination of complete victory in this lifetime. We need to safeguard ourselves against what happened to Elijah. He experienced a victory, but quickly turned it into a defeat. Why?

First, Elijah forgot the power of God. He got overconfident. We do the same thing. God transforms us, and we learn a new way of life. Then we tell God, "Thanks! I can handle it from here." But we can't. Before long, temptation wears us down. Then we revert to an old pattern of living. We relapse, forgetting how God pulled us through. We get overconfident and feel we can go it alone. But then we quickly realize that we can't.

Second, Elijah focused solely on the problem. If you do relapse into old ways of thinking and behaving, stay focused on moving toward your goal, not on the failure of relapse. Focus on recovering from your setbacks. And that's all it is—a setback. We can always move forward by reinitiating a relationship with God based on our powerlessness over our problem.

Third, Elijah isolated himself. He ran away. He escaped and collapsed under a tree with thoughts of failure. It's an easy thing to do, and we do it well. It's easy to hide. But isolation will only make things worse. We need support and encouragement, and we especially need God.

Fourth, Elijah was discouraged. Nothing is going to lead you to a relapse faster than when you allow discouragement to overtake you. I believe that discouragement comes when we start to look at life through the filter of our own strength. Then we hear the whisper of the inner critic: *I knew this wouldn't work out. I knew this was too good to be true. You are hopeless. You will never be able to stay on track.* The inner critic drives us to a deeper sense of self-pity, and this is where our discouragement thrives.

But *God pursued Elijah.* He didn't turn His back in disgust. Instead, God held him accountable. When I was a little boy, I'd run away, and my parents would come and find me. They'd say, "What are you doing here?" and I'd shrug my shoulders. Then lovingly and gently, they guided me home. They wanted me to be safe because they loved me. To me, that is the whole story of the Bible: a loving Father who pursues His children.

In another story, the Prodigal Son squandered his inheritance and lost everything. But when he ventured home, the father didn't punish him. He didn't close off his love. He embraced his son. Loved on him. Threw a party for him. He welcomed him home and cried, "My son who was lost, is now found!"

What wonderful hope for those of us who will relapse! There is a new beginning. But if we turn our relapses into a continuous cycle with clear disregard for the Father's heart and the hearts of those who love us, then we are only playing a game. Eventually everyone will feel we've taken advantage of their love.

It's a long journey, this journey to freedom. The Bible says about this journey: "We have around us many people whose lives tell us what faith means. So let us run the race that is before us and never give up. We should remove from our lives anything that would get in the way and the sin that so easily holds us back."[3] So, be patient. Keep your focus on God. Take it one day at a time. Think of Colonel Sanders. Think of his failures. Then think of what he did with that $105 check.

REFLECTIONS

ONE SET OF CIRCUMSTANCES CAN SET INTO MOTION A DOMINO EFFECT OF GREAT THINGS IN YOUR LIFE.

- Do you ever feel stuck and unable to move forward?

• What do you need to let go of that is keeping you stuck and discouraged?

• Does Colonel Sanders's story offer you hope? If so, how?

RELATIONSHIPS ON THE JOURNEY

An old man walked beside his grandson who rode a donkey as they traveled from one city to another. The old man heard some people say, "Would you look at that old man suffering on his feet while that strong boy is totally capable of walking!"

In the next town, the old man rode the donkey to keep people from thinking badly about his grandson. But then he heard some people saying, "Would you look at that, a healthy man riding a donkey while he makes that poor boy walk!"

This frustrated the man, so he jumped on the donkey behind his grandson. Now both rode the donkey. But then they heard some people say, "Would you look at those heavy brutes making that poor donkey suffer!"

So, they both got off and walked the donkey. But then they heard some people say, "Would you look at that waste—a perfectly good donkey not being used!"

So, the boy and the old man just ended up carrying the donkey.

No matter what you do in life, someone is going to criticize you. Some people just feel compelled to give their opinion on everything, and that's fine. But advice can go in two directions—it can be constructive or destructive. We need to avoid destructive criticism and gravitate toward the constructive, which may mean that sometimes you need to avoid those who only tear you down.

BODY

"Running makes me a child, a child at play . . . find your own self-renewing compulsion, and you will become the person you were meant to be."

—Dr. George Sheehan

Because the majority of our relationships are a choice, we choose certain friends. Some are bad. Some are good. The Bible says, "Do not be fooled: 'Bad friends will ruin good habits.'"[1]

Psychologists Henry Cloud and John Townsend say, "Taking a stand against hurtful things that people do and against the things that are opposed to the life that God wants you to create is one of the most positive spiritual things that you can do. God's way is to stand up against bad things."[2]

First, we need to realize that we may need to change some of our current relationships. We may need to change any relationships that lead us back into our destructive habits. We must disassociate from these people—not because we think we are better than they, but because they may not be good for us. If we've been stuck in a certain lifestyle and a certain pattern for years, one of the greatest dilemmas for us may be to consider cutting off those relationships with the ones who've participated with us in our addictions or destructive habits. But not only are these relationships toxic to our healing, but the separation, no matter how painful it may be, may help *them* discover freedom, as well.

In his book *Personal Best*, Dr. George Sheehan wrote that when he left behind a life of drinking, he became a runner and developed a completely new group of friends who were also involved in running. As his lifestyle changed, so did his group of friends.[3]

Dr. Henry Cloud and Dr. John Townsend write, "Relationships carry power—power to do good or power to do evil."[4] We see this in the life of Joseph in the Bible. Joseph was a handsome Jewish servant and house manager for one of Pharaoh's officials in Egypt. His striking features attracted the official's wife, who tried to seduce Joseph. Slight sexual innuendos began in whispers. Every day she hounded him: "Have sexual relations with me." Though perhaps tempted, every time Joseph said, "No." Then one day when all of the servants were out of the house, she made inappropriate advances toward him him. But Joseph was loyal to his conscience and to God, and when she went for him, he ran. Joseph had the character and the good sense to flee from her.[5]

Sometimes we need to do the same. We need to follow our conscience and remain loyal to God. We need to run from toxic people who try to lead us astray.

Second, there are those who will lead us upward toward our new life, toward the changes that we are trying to bring about in our lives. Find new companions who are on a path to a lifetime of hope, health, and happiness. We need to surround ourselves with these people. We need their support. We need their encouragement. We need their accountability.

Cloud and Townsend believe we need to give and receive the following things: support, love, courage, feedback, wisdom, experience, and accountability. So, how do we give and receive these gifts?

Listening is the greatest gift we can give and receive. Listening encourages open discussion. Never judge someone while you are listening to them. The fact that they are telling you their truth is important, so affirm that in an encouraging, nonjudgmental way. It always helped me when those around me would assure me that I wasn't alone. They made me feel as if they were in this with me for the long haul. Often, the biggest mistake we make trying to help others is forcing them toward action before they are ready.[6] Sometimes we have to allow them to come to the realization themselves.

Communication is vital. We need to make sure we are communicating effectively, and not turning away the people we need to have in our lives. This can be tricky. It's what the husband in the following story faced when he tried communicating with his wife, who was taking a trip around the world. When she got to London, she called home to the United States, and in the course of the conversation, said to her husband, "How's the dog?"

He said, "Aw, the dog's dead."

She said, "The dog's dead?"

"Yeah, the dog's dead."

MIND

"Many people feel personally overwhelmed by constant change. How can you develop self-esteem when you are flooded with fear? Overwhelmed is a state of mind. Being overwhelmed and doing nothing is an easier response than the hard work of thinking through the new demands and claims on your consciousness."

—Dr. Nathanial Branden

"You heartless brute. You know how much I care about that dog, and you suddenly tell me the dog is dead."

"What should I've said?"

"Well, you could've told me the dog was up on the roof. Then when I got over to Paris and called, you could have told me the dog fell off the roof. Then when I got to Rome, you could have told me the dog wasn't feeling very well. Then when I got to Venice, you could have told me the dog had died. . . . Well, how's Mother?"

He said, "She's up on the roof."

Communication sometimes has a way of breaking down between people. Yes, maybe the woman in this story was manipulative in some ways. But the man got it. He adjusted the lines of communication, and so must we, not out of manipulation, but to make sure we're being heard. Sometimes telling someone a story the way Nathan did after King David's sin of adultery can get their attention. (You can read the entire account in 2 Samuel 12:1–10.) Word pictures and stories can communicate powerful truth in an unobtrusive way.

Never make excuses. Until we suffer our own consequences, we won't change. Our shielding and protecting of others and of ourselves never works. Sometimes we need to step out of the way and let God work. He has a plan. So, try not to take on God's role. He is capable of getting both others and us where we need to be.

Become aware of manipulation techniques. Most of us help others because of our own guilt. Manipulators are good at making other people feel guilty and through this, getting you to do what they want. Anytime a manipulator makes you feel guilty about doing or not doing something, take it as a sign to step back a bit. Helping a manipulator because you feel guilty is called *enabling*. He or she knows how to push your buttons. So, just take away the buttons.

Let go of the results. Sometimes we want to fix the lives of others when they should be fixing their own lives. Leading them to self-discovery is part of change, so leave the results to God. There's a great verse in the Bible in which the apostle Paul wrote about change: "I planted the seed, and Apollos watered it. But God is the One who made it grow."[7] We can plant seeds. We can water. But God is in control of growth. This fact takes the timetable away. It places them and us on God's timetable, which eventually births patience. We should never try to fix what only God can repair.

Relationships are difficult—maybe even one of the most decisive factors in our process of change. Our recovery, our healing, our future may very well come down to whom we associate with and how we handle our loved ones. Work hard in establishing good relationships with others and your change will be successful.

BODY

Walking is one of the greatest mood-altering activities of life. A nice brisk thirty-minute walk in the fresh air releases endorphins which create a feeling of calmness and well-being. To me it's the best anti-depressant on God's market.

REFLECTIONS

**WE NEED TO SURROUND OURSELVES WITH
POSITIVE RELATIONSHIPS THAT WILL ENCOURAGE
US TO KEEP MOVING FORWARD TO OUR NEW
LIFE OF HOPE, HEALTH, AND HAPPINESS.**

- Do you believe the people with whom we associate have an effect on our capacity to change?

- Do you believe it's the structure of the program you use or the relationships we make within the structure that help us change the most?

- Do you surround yourself with people who are supporting and encouraging you to keep moving forward in the changes you need to make in your life?

HOPE RESTORED

GETTING FREE OF A SHAMEFUL LIFE

A *Peanuts* cartoon, posted on a ship bulletin board, pictured Charlie Brown and Lucy on a cruise ship. As they stand on the deck, Lucy says, "Life is like this cruise ship, Charlie Brown. Some people take their deck chairs to the front of the ship so they can see where they are going. Other people take their deck chairs to the back of the ship so they can see where they've been. Which one are you, Charlie Brown?"

He answers, "I'm the kind of person who can't get my deck chair open."

Sound familiar? Some of us are stuck in a life that never seems to work. But instead of trying to fix it, we settle for the bargain bin, defeatedly admitting that we are slightly blemished. We discount our lives. We mark down our value. We're stuck because we say, "I'm not worth fixing. I'll always be worthless."

Before my journey toward freedom, I was stuck. It wasn't until I got into a twelve-step program and took action did I change. I needed to take a step. To get unstuck. I needed to do something. It became apparent to me that I was mourning the past. I kept trying to reach back and rearrange things. I wanted the past to be different. But what I didn't realize is that the greatest bondage in life is to be stuck in the past. And from this point of hopelessness comes the attitude of shame. *I keep letting God down, my family down, my friends down, and myself down. I'm so ashamed.*

SPIRIT

"It is not the critic that counts: not the man who points out how the strong man stumbles, or where the doer of deeds could have done better. The credit belongs to the man who is actually in the arena, whose face is marred by dust and sweat and blood, who strives valiantly, who errs, and comes short again and again, because there is no effort without error: but who does actually strive to do good deeds."

—THEODORE ROOSEVELT

In the movie *The Edge,* Charles Morse (Anthony Hopkins) and Robert Green (Alec Baldwin) are stranded in the wilderness following a plane crash. They end up begrudgingly helping each other survive the elements and a series of bear attacks. It's a movie of wonderful dialogue. In one of the best scenes, Morse says, as if addressing their circumstances, "I read an interesting book that said most people lost in the wilderness die of shame. Yeah. See, they die of shame. *What did I do wrong? How could have I gotten myself into this?* So, they sit there and die. Because they didn't do the one thing which would have saved their lives . . . thinking."

Relentless self-criticism always keeps us stuck. Because we don't do the one thing that can get us free— which is to forgive ourselves and think of solutions— we become lost in the wilderness. We sit and die.

There are two ruts of shame that isolate us in our journey. *The first rut is the rut of self-pity.* Søren Kierkegaard once said that all despair is fundamentally a despair of being ourselves. This is the reason so many of us seek change. We are tired of being who we are. We are ashamed of the way we've acted or the way our lives have turned out. But the difference between those who die in their shame and those who transcend it is ultimately a matter of action. One takes action and overcomes. The other becomes stuck in the wilderness of despair and gives up.

Coach Mike Krzyzewski, Duke University basketball coach, tells a story about the year they won the National Championship. Duke played rival North Carolina and lost by a large margin. The bus ride back to Durham late at night was grueling. When the players got off the bus and started to go back to the dorms, Coach Krzyzewski said, "Where are you going? Let's go practice." Unbelievably, the team's best practice of the year came after that loss—and in the middle of the night.

Coach Krzyzewski said, "People have more of a tendency to listen after a loss, or after they make a mistake. The hardest thing is to have them listen when you're winning. That's why sustained excellence is the most difficult thing to achieve, because you feel like you don't need one another for it."[1]

We will all make mistakes and suffer setbacks. Relapse will happen. Dr. James Prochaska, author of *Changing for Good*, prefers the word *recycle*, instead of *relapse*. Dr. Prochaska writes, "Recycling gives us opportunities to learn. Action followed by relapse is far better than no action at all. People who take action and fail in the next month are twice as likely to succeed over the next six months than those who don't take any action at all."[2] This goes back to what we discussed in Day 4 about *training versus trying*. As we contemplate the process of change, we need to realize that there is a good possibility we will *recycle*.[3] Growth usually involves temporary setbacks. There are challenges along the way. The road is bumpy. It's never just a straight line of being on our path and not looking back. We follow a jagged line. But progress *can* happen. We *can* grow through trials and tribulations. Just don't stop. Refuse to fall into self-pity. Keep thinking.

The second rut is the rut of stuffing our pain inside instead of working through it. When we fail horribly or when someone hurts us, we want to disconnect from the pain. So, we stuff it. We cover it with a scab called a *false self*—a scab that can be knocked off with ease. It only takes one mistake, one putdown by another, one lost relationship, and the scab peels away. And what is left is a wounded feeling of shame. Psychologist Karen Horney writes, "We cannot suppress or eliminate essential parts of ourselves without becoming estranged from ourselves. . . . The person simply becomes oblivious to what he really

> ## BODY
>
> "The strong relationship between regular exercise and good health has been established beyond all doubt."
>
> —GEORGE LEONARD AND MICHAEL MURPHY, *THE LIFE WE ARE GIVEN*

feels, likes, rejects, believes—in short, to what he really is. Without knowing it he may live the life of his image."[4]

We think that if people knew the truth about us, they wouldn't like us. So, we pretend we are someone else, and by doing this, we reject our pain. We stuff it instead of dealing with it.

Lewis Smedes says, "Some of us deny the pain we really feel. It just hurts too much to acknowledge it. Sometimes it scares us; people betrayed and brutalized by their parents are often afraid to admit their pain for fear they may hate the people they most dearly want to love."[5] Smedes goes on to say that it's like the betrayed wife who shoves her pain in the dark room of the soul where feelings are not allowed to enter. She says, "I will never let him have the pleasure of seeing me suffer for his little escapade with his secretary." And as long as she refuses to acknowledge her pain, she will never forgive him or feel loved by him. She has closed herself off from healing and intimacy. She has closed herself off from all inner beauty and goodness.

Shame injures our relationships. We cannot experience intimacy if we've closed off our true self. This is why we fall in love with objects. They don't require intimacy. To love houses, cars, jewelry, and other stuff is a false intimacy that never fulfills our loneliness. But we believe if we can just get more and more stuff that it will finally be enough one day. It never is. Objects can never provide the intimacy that we crave so desperately. Relating to the world on this level never makes us feel loved for who we are, but for how we look, how we perform, or by what we own. This defense mechanism helps for a while. But eventually we get tired of the charades. It wears us down.

If you feel lost in the wilderness, or like Charlie Brown, who couldn't get his deck chair open, then try to get on the solution side of the problem.

Think. Think of ways to overcome. Think of solutions. The answer may be inside you instead of from some outside source.

Don't allow your problems to become permanent. Think your way out. Find solutions. Team up with others. Let them help you, because the biggest mistake in the process of change is giving up. We must believe change is possible.

If you relapse, don't let it plunge you into shame. Instead, use the setback by learning from it. This causes our heart to be receptive to listening to God. He is always teaching us better ways, but when we think we can do it without Him, we fail. So, take some time to reflect on your situation. Listen for God to direct you. This turns the focus away from us. It makes us receptive to change. Try it. You can overcome!

REFLECTIONS

SELF-CRITICISM ALWAYS KEEPS US STUCK.

ONE THING THAT CAN FREE US FROM SELF-CRITICISM IS TO FORGIVE OURSELVES FOR OUR MISTAKES.

- If Lucy in the *Peanuts* cartoon asked you what type of person you are in the same context she asked Charlie Brown, how would you respond?

• If people knew the truth about you, would they like you? Why or why not?

• Do you believe you have a "false self"? Why or why not?

THE PURSUIT OF GOD

Mars Incorporated, the maker of Snickers candy bars, has a humorous commercial that portrays a crotchety and vindictive God seated behind a massive desk on a fluffy cloud in heaven. Stretched out in front of the huge desk is a line of people of all sizes and races. At the front of the line, God is pounding a small man with accusation after accusation about his sinful life. At each accusation, the man winces. In the middle of the line, a young, impatient man steps out and yells, "Does this line ever move?" Suddenly a hole opens in the cloud, the man drops through, and God says, "It's moving now."

In a humorous way, this commercial reveals what most people believe about God. They believe He is a cantankerous judge, long on fire and brimstone and short on patience. Some believe heaven is a long line leading to eternal judgment, according to our behavior on earth. It is hard to trust a vindictive God when we hold this type of agenda. No one wants a relationship with an abusive God.

Discovering God can be a confusing subject because our ideas about God can keep us from trusting Him. Theologian Os Guinness writes in his book *God in the Dark,* "But if our picture of God is wrong, then our whole presupposition of what it is possible for God to be or do is correspondingly altered. . . . Faith is out of focus, God is not seen as he is . . . [and] doubt easily grows. Such doubts are the direct result of a faulty picture of God."[1]

A faulty view will keep us from having a relationship with God. It will keep us from becoming who we were meant to be—children of God.

SPIRIT

"We are not accustomed to thinking that God's will for us and our own inner dreams can coincide. Instead, we have bought the message of our culture: This world is a veil of tears, and we are meant to be dutiful and die. The truth is: We are to be bountiful and live."

—Julia Cameron,
The Artist Way

In Day 19, I discussed how stuffing the pain leads to the development of a false self. So, the key to healing is to try to heal the wound of shame and therefore discover our true selves. We can do this in two ways.

First, we can discover our true self by having a relationship with God. God's power is not a petulant force or some kind of harsh judgment. It's a relationship. And as we get to know Him more, His life bleeds into ours, the way it does when we fall in love with another human being. We take on His mannerisms. We live to please Him. We want to be with Him. We want to be like Him. This is how we take on His power. There's more to it than just believing in a higher power. It's a relationship. We accept His love, and He becomes not just an idea or some magical genie to transport us out of our lousy circumstances. He becomes our ultimate Friend and Traveling Companion along our journey to healing.

Understanding God in this way has been the greatest experience of my life. I realize that He might not change all of my circumstances. But I know He'll always be with me on my journey. So, I let Him teach me and guide me. This is intimacy with God. And all of us crave it. But it is impossible to have intimacy without being vulnerable and honest. I can't be honest with you or with myself if I feel like I'm standing before a furious judge. I'll cover my inadequacies by using my false self, even believing that I can somehow trick God.

Christ said, "Then you will know the truth, and the truth will make you free" (John 8:32). And this is what we are trying to get at—the truth. The truth that we cannot do this on our own. The truth that we are creatures created for God's friendship. We get to the truth by being honest with God and ourselves. We seek a relationship. Then the true self emerges.

Second, we can discover that intimacy with God is the realization that we are valued and loved by God—even when we may feel or be unlovable. When we feel loved in spite of ourselves, it frees us to be more loving toward others. This is why Christ said of the prostitute who washed His feet with her tears and dried them with her hair, "I tell you that her many sins are forgiven, so she showed great love. But the person who is forgiven only a little will love only a little."[2]

God does not love us because we are good, but He will make us good because He loves us. Intimacy with God occurs when we acknowledge all of our imperfections before Him.

It's impossible to see the truth about ourselves without the help of God. Only God's Word can get to the center of our souls and heal us. "God's word is alive and working and is sharper than a double-edged sword. It cuts all the way into us, where the soul and the spirit are joined, to the center of our joints and bones. And it judges the thoughts and feelings in our hearts."[3] When God speaks to me through the Bible or through another person, I see the truth about myself, about who I really am, about what I have been doing. But unlike the God in the Snickers commercial, God loves me and forgives me, and He begins to reveal a way out of my isolation and brokenness. He leads me to a life of freedom.

It's impossible to have intimacy without being vulnerable. I can't be honest with God or with someone else if I don't risk vulnerability. I will continue to hide behind the false self—never risking and never knowing intimacy. We can isolate ourselves from God even in church. We can be at a Bible study, but be very distant from God. We can appear religious. We see this in the case of the Pharisees, the religious scholars of Jesus' day. Jesus said of them, "How terrible for you, teachers of the law and Pharisees! You are hypocrites! You are like tombs that are painted white. Outside, those tombs look fine, but inside, they

> # MIND
>
> "When we think of happiness, we should not focus on our needs so much as our possibilities, we are unhappy not because of things we lack but because we have potentialities that have not been realized."
>
> —Dr. George Sheehan, *Personal Best*

are full of the bones of dead people and all kinds of unclean things."[4] Jesus was hard on the Pharisees. He showed more mercy to a prostitute caught in the act of adultery than He did to them. He hated fake religiosity. Still does. Always will. Authenticity and vulnerability matter to God.

My vulnerability started in recovery when I began to drop my false self. I realized I could be myself with flaws and all. That was the greatest feeling in my life. Then I was open to change. It made me want to be a better person.

Trusting God is the first step toward vulnerability. When we trust Him, it doesn't mean we will not fail. It doesn't mean that He is a grandfather in the sky who wants us to know only bliss. Life will still be difficult. We will fail. This is what vulnerability is all about—the freedom to make mistakes and learn. It's like the young new president of a bank who made an appointment with his predecessor to seek advice. He began, "Sir, as you well know, I lack a great deal of qualifications you already have for this job. You have been very successful as president of this bank, and I wondered if you would be kind enough to share with me some of the insights you have gained from your years here that have been the keys to your success."

The older man looked at him with a stare and replied: "Young man, two words: *good decisions.*"

The young man responded, "Thank you very much, sir, but how does one come to know which is the good decision?"

"One word, young man: *experience.*"

"But how does one get experience?"

"Two words, young man: *bad decisions.*"

Vulnerability is nothing more than gaining *experience* walking with a God who knows that *experience* is everything. He doesn't expect us to be perfect. He only desires progress, and making progress comes down to trial and error. The one constant in all of it is the love of God. He understands, like the older bank president, and He doesn't expect us to know everything about what a relationship with Him looks like. He knows that good decisions are a result of some bad decisions. God is not looking for a perfect person. He only desires a relationship that is genuine and vulnerable, and out of this type of relationship, intimacy can happen. When intimacy becomes the basis of a relationship with God, where we share everything in a vulnerable way with God, then we can't help but change.

REFLECTIONS

DISCOVERING GOD CAN BE CONFUSING.

FAULTY IDEAS ABOUT GOD CAN KEEP US FROM TRUSTING HIM. TO HAVE A REAL AND POWERFUL RELATIONSHIP WITH GOD, WE NEED TO DISPROVE THESE FAULTY IDEAS.

- Do you believe intimacy with God is the beginning of intimacy with ourselves?

- Do you feel valued and loved by God?

- Are you experiencing a level of intimacy in the key relationships in your life?

A CASE OF MISTAKEN IDENTITY

A college student needed a small two-hour course to fill his schedule. The only one that fit into his schedule was a course in Wildlife Zoology. He had some reservations about the course because he had heard it was tough and the teacher was a bit quirky. But it seemed like the only choice, so he signed up.

After one week and one chapter, the professor gave the class a test. He passed out a sheet of paper divided into squares. In each square was a carefully drawn picture of some bird legs. Not bodies, not wings, not colors, not locales—only bird legs. The students had to identify the birds from the pictures of their legs.

It shocked the student. He didn't have a clue as to what the answers were. The student stared at the test and grew angrier and angrier. Finally reaching the boiling point, he stomped up to the front of the classroom, threw the test on the teacher's desk, and exclaimed, "This is the worst test I've ever seen, and this is the dumbest course I've ever taken."

The teacher looked up at him and said, "Young man, you just flunked the test." Then the teacher picked up the student's paper, saw that he hadn't put his name on it, and asked, "By the way, young man, what's your name?"

At this the student bent over, pulled up his pants, revealed his legs, and said, "You identify me!"

Identity is at the heart of changing our life. Identifying the future, identifying true friends, identifying our weaknesses, and identifying our true selves are all important factors. *Who am I?* Most of us define ourselves by the world's standards. But our true identity is stamped on the soul from within. We have to do the work of discovering our true selves.

Jane Fonda calls the false self "disembodiment." In her book *My Life So Far,* she writes, "Because I believed that to be loved I had to be perfect, I moved 'out of myself'—my body—early on and have spent much of my life searching to come home . . . to be embodied. I didn't understand this until I was in my 60s and started writing this book. I have come to believe that my purpose in life may be to show—through my own story—how this 'disembodiment' happens and how, by understanding it, we can change."[1]

When we look to others to give us an identity, there will be those who will attempt to control us. And then, we are either up or down according to how the controller is treating us. When they treat us well, we feel good about ourselves. But the problem is, we are allowing someone else to do the work we should be doing on our own. This breeds insecurity and encourages the false self to grow. The Bible says, "Do not change yourselves to be like the people of this world, but be changed within by a new way of thinking. Then you will be able to decide what God wants for you; you will know what is good and pleasing to him and what is perfect."[2]

The turning point for Jane Fonda happened in 1998. She made a twenty-minute documentary about her life as a sixtieth birthday present to herself. As she reflected on her life, she had a realization: "The disease to please was in me from an early age."[3]

Many of us become addicted to people-pleasing. We expend incredible energy always trying to be perfect. But it's like holding a balloon underwater—eventually a problem is going to come up. When we feel like a failure, and we run to something to medicate our feelings of inferiority, we are stuffing our emotions. Emotions have to go somewhere—and whether they channel themselves through an eating disorder, alcoholism, or codependency, they will manifest themselves somehow in our lives. We can't hold it together forever. For Jane Fonda, her struggle with identity manifested itself through bulimia.

In my own recovery, one of the saddest moments of my life was when I realized how dishonest I was and how much deceit, how much pretense, made up my life. I was afraid of being alone. I so wanted to be with someone whom I trusted and who understood me. But when our insecurities cause us to move out of ourselves and "disembody"—as Fonda refers to it—then we become a stranger to ourselves.

When I entered recovery, I had no inner identity. I didn't know who I was. But I knew that I craved companionship with someone who would love me. However, I learned that I couldn't really love another person until I first identified and loved myself. It sounds so selfish, I know. But, really, it isn't—it is self-acceptance. All of us live with our actual selves and our ideal selves. There's a tension between who we are and who we want to become. The civil war in our souls is our effort to reconcile the two. And how we deal with this reconciliation is usually where our problems emerge. If we fail to live up to our ideals, we plunge into a devastating sense of inferiority where insecurities abound: *I'm not lovable. I'm worthless.*

Dr. Harry Emerson Fosdick, in his book *On Being a Real Person,* says there are three unhealthy ways to deal with a sense of inferiority: 1) the smokescreen method, 2) the sour-grapes method, and 3) the fantasy method.[4]

Feelings of inferiority cause us to surround ourselves with smokescreens in an effort to hide who we really are. In order to lead people away from our feelings of inferiority, we trump up our life with false accomplishments. We walk around as if we are an advertisement for narcissism. We brag. We tell lies. We con people. All in an attempt to cover our inferiorities. But don't be deceived. Everyone can usually see right through the smokescreen. And by covering up

> # BODY
>
> "But the real juice of life is to be found not nearly so much in the products of our efforts as in the process of living itself, in how it feels to be alive."
>
> —GEORGE LEONARD AND
> MICHAEL MURPHY,
> *THE LIFE WE ARE GIVEN*

our inferiority, we isolate ourselves. We drive people away. No one wants to listen to a narcissist.

Others use the sour-grape method, the way the fox did in Aesop's fable. The fox called everything he could not reach, "sour grapes." Fosdick writes, "Watch what people are cynical about, and one can often discover what they lack, and subconsciously, beneath their touchy condescension, deeply wish they had."[5]

Others deal with their inferiority by using fantasy to escape. Unable to fulfill their idealized image, they retreat to a life of fantasy, where everything they wish comes true without the threat of failure. But the danger of fantasy is that it can become more vivid than reality. This is how people get caught up in Internet porn, excessive gambling, extramarital affairs, and drugs that make us forget about ourselves. We involve ourselves in fantasy because we want to escape reality. In fantasy, everything is selfish and safe. Then it becomes so vivid that we begin to play these fantasies out in reality. Fantasy can apply to anything that can become an excessive daydream.

Self-acceptance allows us to be at peace with who we are. We might as well be at peace because, no matter how hard we try, we can't escape ourselves. If we try, we land in the unhealthy areas we mentioned previously. Alcibiades, a gifted but unscrupulous Greek, was noted as an unhappy man. Someone asked Socrates why it was that Alcibiades, who had traveled so much and had seen so much of the world, was still an unhappy man. Socrates answered, "Because wherever he goes, he always takes himself."

Another benefit of self-acceptance is the quality of our relationships. Intimacy increases dramatically in relationships when both people are aware and accepting of themselves. As I continue to evolve from my false self into my authentic self, I'm discovering that I can enter relationships without trying to overcompensate to make you love me. I've discovered the true meaning of intimacy, and I'm not going to wither away and die if you choose to reject me. I'm going to be okay. Now I enter relationships from a place of abundance. I have something to give away. This is freedom—freedom to be happy even when I take myself with me on the journey.

REFLECTIONS

**IDENTITY IS AT THE HEART OF CHANGING OUR LIVES.
IDENTIFYING THE FUTURE, IDENTIFYING TRUE FRIENDS,
IDENTIFYING OUR WEAKNESSES, AND IDENTIFYING
OUR TRUE SELVES ARE ALL IMPORTANT FACTORS.**

- Can we find our identity by winning the approval of others? Why or why not?

- Do you need the approval of others to validate your self-worth?

- Dr. Harry Emerson Fosdick, in his book *On Being a Real Person*, says there are three unhealthy ways to deal with a sense of inferiority: 1) the smokescreen method, 2) the sour-grapes method, and 3) the fantasy method. Which method do you use?

COURAGE IS OUR GREATNESS

Blues Boy had no indication that this song would be any different. His first seven recordings had flopped, and recording his latest song at the vacant room at the Abe Scharff YMCA in Memphis, Tennessee, didn't add much hope. If anything, it called for even more courage. The recording was cheap and simple—no editing available. It was taped in mono with no room for error, meaning that if Blues Boy and his band messed up, the Ampec reel-to-reel had to start over from the beginning. But, despite the pressure, it only took them two takes to record "Three O'Clock Blues." The song went on to become Blues Boy's first national hit. It remained at number one on Billboard's rhythm-and-blues chart for three months, and from the vacant room in the Memphis YMCA on Lauderdale and Vance, Blues Boy became the man and the legend known as B. B. King.

B. B. said of the song being number one on the rhythm-and-blues chart: "That changed my life."[1]

None of us knows when something will come along and change our lives. But B. B. King's recording in the vacant room at the Y proves that sometimes the most unlikely thing in the most implausible place can become a success. If B. B. King had given up after the first seven flops, he would've remained unknown to this day.

Unfortunately, most of us give up before we reach a breakthrough. In

America, we spend an estimated $30 billion per year on unsuccessful attempts to sustain a healthy lifestyle. It's astonishing! Why are so many people failing? I believe it has to do with a lack of courage.

Recently I've come to a fuller understanding of courage. When I was young, my definition of courage embodied movie stars like Clint Eastwood and John Wayne. These men faced down bullets in ambushes, in taverns, in rain that raked the streets and pelted their gallon-sized cowboy hats. These men never complained about the coffee that was so un-Starbucks-like. They sat around campfires, drinking and talking, ready to put their hands on their pistols to fight things that made their horses whinny in the night. Scared of nothing. Makers of destiny. And I would walk across my lawn with a John Wayne stride, imagining I was on my way to find the joker who'd just killed someone in cold blood. Looking into the eyes of these big-screen cowboys instantly convinced me that courage could overcome evil. Their far-fetched stories, long on courage and short on defeat, converted me as they flickered on the movie screens of my childhood.

As I look back over my life as an adult, I wouldn't consider myself a very courageous person. Many times, I've cowered in fear and retreated from confrontation. I was the classic passive-aggressive person who held deep resentment toward others, and then would suddenly blow up and cause great damage to my relationships. I lacked the courage to stand my ground and speak the truth. So, as we look at changing our lives, let's define *courage*. Someone once said that courage is like a tea bag; you never know the strength of it until it's put in hot water.

In the movie, *Men of Honor*—the true-story account of Carl Brashear becoming the first black Navy deep-sea diver—there's an early scene in which his father is plowing a field with a mule and plow. His hands are bloody. His life is tough. It would be Carl's life, too, if he stayed on the farm. But Carl follows

BODY

Age is irrelevant. You can build muscle and bone mass at any age. Research shows that big gains in muscle mass can be acquired until age 60. Moderate amounts until age 100!

SPIRIT

"Truly, it is in the darkness that one finds the light, so when we are in sorrow, then this light is nearest of all to us."

—NEISTER ECKHART

his dream of becoming a diver, and when his parents take him to the bus station, his father tells him, "Don't you come back here, and it's gonna get hard, and it will be hard." His father knows that the hardest part will be for Carl to keep a resilient spirit. Great courage resides in a resilient spirit. A resilient spirit is one that keeps stepping up to the challenge, forgetting the past and forging ahead. This is why this scene in this movie resonates with me. I believe God is trying to instill in us a resilient spirit. He wants us to face down our challenges. As Carl's father said, "It's gonna get hard, and it will be hard."

Dietrich Bonhoeffer, the great German theologian hanged by Hitler for his repudiation of the Nazis, wrote in a letter while in prison, "I believe God will give us all the power we need to resist in all time of distress. But he never gives it in advance, lest we should rely upon it ourselves and not him."[2] This is true courage—to wait upon God's power. Spiritual courage is not cowboy courage. None of us are spiritual John Waynes. We only become courageous as we understand the power of God within us.

A WINNIE-THE-POOH KIND OF DAY

Years ago, early in my journey to freedom, self-doubt and insecurities plagued my efforts to change. Everything I wanted to believe seemed false. It was a feeling that somehow God's grace had limitations when it came to my recovery. I was on the verge of relapse. So, I went for a walk at nearby Radnor Lake, along the beautiful trails where the lake is nestled inside the city. I always liked to time my hike so I'd be at the peak of a certain ridge at sunset. This particular hike took place in the fall. The leaves were golden, and the sun radiated on the lake. I needed this inspirational atmosphere. I was beginning to wonder if God really cared about my struggles. Then suddenly I turned a bend in the trail, and a doe and two baby fawns met me. The four of us stood and looked at each other for the longest moment. God spoke to my spirit and said, *Do you see the two baby fawns? They're not fearful, because they know their mother will not abandon them. She will die to protect them.* It was like God was saying, *Scott, have courage. I am with you, and I will always be with you.* It gave me such a feeling of resilience.

The day after this hike, I received a card in the mail from a friend. On the front was an illustration of Winnie-the-Pooh and Piglet walking down a winding country road. Piglet is reaching up to take Pooh's hand, and in the caption Piglet says, "I just needed to know you were there."

FEAR NO EVIL

Perseverance in spite of everything is the face of courage. What motivated B. B. King to walk into that vacant room and sing with such emotion? He said, "When I sang 'Three O'Clock Blues,' I was thinking of how much I loved Lowell Fulson's version, but how I also wanted to put my own hurting on that beautiful song."[3] This is a beautiful depiction of our relationship with God. It's what Bonhoeffer was saying through his prison bars. All of us need to put "our own hurting" on God. This may be the greatest courage. To let go. To rip our idolatrous hands off of ourselves. The apostle Paul said not long before his death, "My life is being given as an offering to God, and the time has come for me to leave this life. I have fought the good fight, I have finished the race, I have kept the faith."[4] This is courage—to give ourselves to God, to fight to the end, to remain faithful, knowing He walks with us in this valley of the shadow of death. We will fear nothing.

REFLECTIONS:

GREAT COURAGE RESIDES IN A RESILIENT SPIRIT,
AS WE KEEP STEPPING UP TO THE CHALLENGE,
FORGETTING THE PAST, AND FORGING AHEAD.

• Do trials and tribulations make you weak, or do you respond instead with great courage?

• How do you increase courage?

• Do we become more courageous as we understand the power of God within us?

THE PROMISE OF HOPE

During World War II, the Nazis set up a camp factory in Hungary where prisoners were made to labor surrounded by barbaric conditions. One day the prisoners were ordered to move a huge pile of garbage from one end of the camp to another. The next day, they were ordered to move the pile back to its original location. No reason was given; they were just told to do it. So began a pattern. Day after day, the prisoners hauled the same mountain of garbage from one end of the camp to the other.

The impact on the prisoners of that mindless, meaningless labor and existence began to come to the surface. One day an elderly prisoner began sobbing uncontrollably and had to be led away. Then another man began screaming until he was beaten into silence. A third man, who had endured three years of labor in the camp, suddenly broke away and began running toward the electric fence. He was told to stop or he would be electrocuted. He didn't care. He flung himself on the fence and died in a blinding flash.

In the days that followed, dozens of prisoners went insane. Their captors didn't care, for what the prisoners didn't know was that they were part of an experiment in mental health. The Nazis wanted to determine what would happen when people were subjected to meaningless activity. They wanted to see what a life would become without a sense of purpose. They concluded that

MIND

"Hope requires strength—sometimes all the strength you can muster. But hope also gives you strength. Hope energizes. hope moves you forward. When you dare to hope, you can do so much more than you ever thought."

—EMILIE BARNES,
THE PROMISES OF HOPE

the result was insanity and suicide. The commandant even remarked that at the rate prisoners were killing themselves, there would no longer be a need to use the gas chambers.

Meaning is decisive to human existence. We all need a purpose. We need to know that our lives matter. This is why God says, "I know what I am planning for you. . . . I have good plans for you, not plans to hurt you. I will give you hope and a good future."[1] Hope is so important to our future. And the great thing about hope is that God gives it freely. He has a purpose for our lives.

Hope is an outgrowth of faith, for faith is believing in what we cannot see. We can't touch hope. We can't hear it or feel it. It's like the wind. It's like the atoms and molecules that make up our world. It's like television waves and radio waves. You can't see them, but they are all around you. So, hope is created by our faith.

Lewis Smedes says there are three things going on inside us whenever we hope for something: "The first is desire; we want what we hope for. The second is belief; we believe that what we hope for is possible. The third is doubt; we fear that what we hope for may not happen."[2] Let's take a look at each one of these statements.

First, we need to realize that desire means wanting what we hope for. Everyone wants something. We want our bills paid. We want our children to stay off drugs. We want a nice house in the suburbs or a bungalow at the beach. We want a better job. We want to remain beautiful as we age. We want to lose weight. We want to become addiction-free. We want to be a better person. So, how do we get what we hope for? It's simple. We must first desire change to the point that we begin to prepare to take action to obtain a new lifestyle. If we want to hit a home run in baseball, we must first get into the game. We desire it, and so we join a team.

At this point on the journey to freedom, you hopefully have identified your problem area, so here's a brief self-assessment to help you gauge your progress so far in the process of change. Check the statements below that are true.

1. _____ I've told one other person about my desire to change.
2. _____ I'm committed to doing whatever it takes to change my lifestyle.
3. _____ I now realize the impact my destructive patterns have had on my life.
4. _____ I'm willing to get an accountability partner to help me.
5. _____ I'm willing to take the next step and write an action plan at the end of this six-week study to help me change my lifestyle.

Some of you are at different stages than others. Some of you may have checked the first three, but not the last two. This is honesty. But understand, your desires will only come true when you are able to check all five as true statements. And you may not be there yet. That's okay. That's normal. Work your way through at your own pace. But make sure you don't fall into a perpetual state of wishful thinking, where all you do is discuss your desires. Eventually we have to get up to bat and swing at the ball if we want to hit a home run. If we want a new job, then we have to prepare a résumé and send it out. If we want to meet new people, we have to emerge from our isolation.

Second, we have to believe that what we hope for is possible. If we fall into hopelessness, then the next stage is self-pity or depression. Maybe both. Lewis Smedes writes, "Hope builds on possibilities."[3] So, start with one step of faith. Take baby steps. You don't have to do it all in one week. Make some small goals, and then accomplish those goals. As you accomplish each one, it will give you more hope. This is what Smedes means when he says, "Hope builds on possibilities."

I hit the lowest point in my life when I went through my divorce at about forty years of age. I looked at everything about myself, and there was not one

MIND

"No matter what your situation, it is your task to set priorities and realistically decide what is possible and what is not possible for yourself. Discipline yourself to focus on what must be done, rather than on your self-doubt. Most people who avoid surrendering to panic are able to see what they are capable of."
—DR. NATHANIAL BRANDEN

good thought, so I eventually stopped looking for anything good. I was depressed. Full of self-pity. I couldn't imagine how I was going to pick up the pieces and move forward. But the one strand of hope that I had was to believe that something outside of my own strength could change me. This kind of hope produced the most honest prayer that I have ever prayed to God. It began as a small voice crying out for help, and then the potential for change began, even when all my logic told me that my life was ruined. Over time, God proved my logic to be all wrong.

Third, we have to realize that hope itself has an element of doubt in it. This seems to go against everything I just said, but it really doesn't. If it is possible for us to swing at the ball, then there's the possibility that we might strike out. As Lewis Smedes says, "Human hope is always a risk."[4] We must believe and doubt at the same time. There's the possibility that the pitcher may throw four balls over our head. But this doesn't mean that we stop going up to bat. Just because we hope for something, it doesn't mean it will happen on our timetable.

Some of us stop stepping up to the plate because too many things have happened in the past. We've struck out more times than we've gotten a base hit. So, we just give up on the home run. Did you know that Babe Ruth led the American League in strikeouts for six years of his career? But he knew that to get a home run, he had to swing. So, hope is a risk. But we must never stop hoping.

As I am writing this book, both of my parents are suffering through extremely tough times. My dad is seventy-eight years old and battling cancer and heart problems. My mother has the onset of Alzheimer's. All of my children are grown and living in other cities, so I'm struggling with the empty-nest syndrome. It makes me very sad when I embrace these things. I want my parents to remain strong and youthful. I miss my children, and each time I pass their rooms, sadness comes into my heart. It makes me remember the Serenity Prayer: "God grant me the serenity to accept the things I cannot change, the courage to change the things I can, and wisdom to know the difference."

W. Paul Jones, writing in an article published in *Weavings—Woven Together in Love—A Journal of the Christian Spiritual Life,* says that the root word of *courage* is *heart.*[5] So, *courage* means acting from a hopeful, trusting heart. Then Jones gives a superb illustration of how often life will try to beat us down. The example comes from Ernest Hemingway's *The Old Man and the Sea.* In the story, Hemingway's main character, an old fisherman, has always wanted to catch a huge fish, and finally one day—when he is all alone—he catches it. His hands are bloody from the rope. His body works against the fish. Finally, after he subdues the fish, he realizes that the fish is larger than his boat. He has no choice but to tow the fish back to land. Suddenly, a shark appears and goes after his catch. The old fisherman watches helplessly as the shark eats his fish. Now all the proof is gone. No one will ever believe he had landed the biggest fish of his life.

Jones believes more is at stake than the fish in this story. There's a courageous perseverance there in spite of everything that went wrong. Even though nothing of value is left of the fish, the old man is faithful to the end. This is what I think about when I visit my parents. I remember how hopeful and faithful they have been in their lives, and even though the human condition has brought sickness upon them, there's still a courageous perseverance. It's a hope that this world is not the end of our existence. As Jones believes, more is at stake than the fish. The Bible says, "If our hope in Christ is for this life only, we should be pitied more than anyone else in the world."[6] This world is not the end. But we've been conditioned our whole lives to believe that the American dream is the "happily ever after." Then we reach an age when we realize that the American dream is more like vapor on a highway. The closer we get to it, the more we understand that there has to be something greater, something more at stake.

Even if a shark consumes our gallant effort in the end, we don't give up. We stay hopeful to the end, no matter what. Because hope responds even when the outcome is dismal.

So, begin to set some small goals. Each time you achieve one, it will build up your hope. It will provide meaning and purpose. The Bible says, "You will feel safe because there is hope; you will look around and rest in safety."[7]

Hope is all about new beginnings. It's about believing in the plan God has for us. We have a hope and a future.

REFLECTIONS

MEANING IS DECISIVE TO HUMAN EXISTENCE. WE ALL NEED A PURPOSE. WE NEED TO KNOW THAT OUR LIVES MATTER. THIS IS WHY GOD SAYS, "I KNOW WHAT I AM PLANNING FOR YOU. . . . I HAVE GOOD PLANS FOR YOU, NOT PLANS TO HURT YOU. I WILL GIVE YOU HOPE AND A GOOD FUTURE."

- How did you score on the brief self-assessment on page 135? Did it reveal anything to you?

• If you could take one baby step toward change, what would it be?

• Do you possess a courageous perseverance in spite of everything? What would it take for you to have this type of perseverance?

REFORMATION VERSUS TRANSFORMATION

A leading business school did a study that showed that its graduates did well at first, but in ten years, a more streetwise, pragmatic group overtook them. The conclusion, according to the professor who ran the study, was simple: "We taught them how to solve problems, not recognize opportunities."[1]

Recovery is about solving problems, but it's also about new opportunities. Once we've emptied out the old life, a new lifestyle should take its place. We never replace one habit for another. If we stop overeating, but begin to smoke, we have only reformed one habit by replacing it with another. This is not freedom. It's called reformation. Dr. Gerald May writes, "Reformation of behavior usually involves *substituting* one addiction for another, adapting to a new, possibly less destructive normality. Sometimes substitution is intentional, sometimes unconscious. An overeater adapts to jogging and yoga; a smoker adapts to chewing gum or eating; a television addict becomes dependent upon guided meditations."[2]

Transformation is the direct opposite of what Dr. May described as reformation. Transformation makes all things new. It's a break from an addiction without replacing it with a substitute. It's the subject of Christ's parable about an evil spirit being cast out and trying to return to the clean house. Christ said:

When an evil spirit comes out of a person, it travels through dry places, looking for a place to rest, but it doesn't find it. So the spirit says, I will go back to the house I left.'When the spirit comes back, it finds the house still empty, swept clean, and made neat. Then the evil spirit goes out and brings seven other spirits even more evil than it is, and they go in and live there. So the person has even more trouble than before. It is the same way with the evil people who live today.[3]

> ## BODY
>
> It is never too late to benefit from beoming active. Independent of my situation in life and my age, my health will benefit from becoming active and my life will be better.

G. Campbell Morgan wrote about Christ's parable, "Reformation is ultimately of no value alone. It is only preparation for worse desolation. The only possible cure for a person [is] the incoming of the new Lord and Master."[4] We dispose of a destructive habit and replace it with the Spirit of Christ. We build a relationship with Him and allow Him to fill the empty spot by asking Him into this void.

In the movie *The Shawshank Redemption*, Andy Dufresne (Tim Robbins) serves two consecutive life terms in prison—wrongly accused of killing his wife. Andy's determination to escape prison hides behind a stoic demeanor. Only fellow inmate Red (Morgan Freeman) knows what's behind Andy's submissive facade. As the days grind on in a brutal atmosphere, Andy begins to trust Red enough to tell him about his plans to escape. He instructs Red—if Red gets out on parole—to go to a certain tree in a field, and there he will find a box of cash for him to use to meet Andy in Mexico. Red sees it as a pipe dream—a fantasy that will probably never happen. Then, one day, Andy makes good on his word and escapes.

After Red's successful parole, he realizes that life as a free man is difficult. He even thinks about committing a crime so he'll be sent back to prison. Red doesn't know how to fill the emptiness of not being incarcerated anymore. He needs a new "normal." He has to make the switch from prison life to civilian

SPIRIT

"The call of God is the expression of God's nature, not ours. God providentially weaves the thread of His call through our lives and only we can distinguish them."

—OSWALD CHAMBERS,
MY UTMOST FOR HIS HIGHEST

life. He feels lost about how to do this, so he thinks about going back to what he had. To him, prison life seems better than the emptiness he feels. He even contemplates suicide. Then Red remembers Andy's words and begins to ask some new questions: *What if Andy was telling the truth? What if there really is a place in Mexico beside the Pacific Ocean where I can live? What if Andy is right?*

And so he decides to find out. Under the tree, inside the box, Red discovers Andy's letter. It reads, "If you've come this far, maybe you are willing to come a little further. . . Remember, Red, hope is a good thing, maybe the best of things, and no good thing ever dies."

This is the whole message of God. He says it to all of us: "If you've come this far, maybe you are willing to come a little further."

In the last scene of the movie, Red rides a bus with his head out of the window, on his way to the blue Pacific Ocean, on his way to a new life. We hear his thoughts as he says, "I find I am so excited I can barely sit still or hold a thought in my head. I think it is the excitement that only a free man can feel, a free man at the start of a long journey whose conclusion is uncertain. I hope I can make it across the border, I hope to see my friend and shake his hand, I hope the Pacific is as blue as it has been in my dreams, I hope." Red put his thoughts into action. He boarded the bus. He left prison life behind. He was transformed by hope. He didn't go back to the bondage of prison life. He discovered freedom—and so can you. Don't settle for a mere swapping of one addiction for another. Fill the emptiness left by the removal of addiction with the Spirit of Christ. Christ didn't come to earth to improve men, but to remake them: "If anyone belongs to Christ, there is a new creation. The old things have gone; everything is made new!"[5] We can leave our prisons behind.

REFLECTIONS

**TRANSFORMATION MAKES ALL THINGS NEW. IT'S A BREAK FROM
AN ADDICTION WITHOUT REPLACING IT WITH A SUBSTITUTE.**

• Have you ever replaced one bad habit for one just as bad—or worse?

• Have you ever felt lost and out of place, like the character Red felt after being released from prison?

• Do you think there is a correlation between overcoming an addiction and being freed from prison? If yes, how? If no, why not?

OVERCOME OBSTACLES

THE POWER OF SMALL GROUPS

According to a forest folktale, two porcupines in Northern Canada huddled together to get warm. But their quills pricked each other, so they moved apart. Before long they were shivering, so they moved back together. But soon both were getting jabbed again. Same story; same ending. They *needed* each other, but they kept *needling* each other.

Living life together with others is not easy. But we learn, as the porcupines learned, that we need each other despite the needling, and small groups provide powerful life-transforming experiences.

A few years ago, Restore Ministries planned some small twelve-step groups for inmates at a local prison to help them overcome various problems. I will never forget the chaplain's response to our program. She said that other organizations do short-term work in the prison, which is needed and is much appreciated, but it's only a one-time presentation where inmates are asked, "Who wants to change?" and the inmates raise their hands. But then the presenters leave and have no more contact with the inmates, and it doesn't take long for the inmates to slip back into their old ways. So, the chaplain was thrilled that we were going to aid the other organizations by forming small groups and building ongoing relationships with the inmates. The chaplain understood the powerful dynamics of a small group, which could provide support, encouragement, hope, accountability, love, and nurturing kindness.

MIND

"It is hope that
maintains most
of mankind."

—SOPHOCLES

(496–406 B.C.)

At Restore, we provide different groups for different needs, such as a twelve-step *Power to Choose* group, a *Love Is a Choice* group for those struggling with co-dependency and destructive patterns in relationships, and a group for those desiring weight loss and more active lifestyles. But in the end, the structure of the group doesn't transform lives. The relationships formed within the group's structure provide strength for the members to change. Relationships keep us on the journey and encourage us when we become weak.

When we feel accepted in a group—flaws and all—we will have a tendency to come out of isolation and work consistently toward change. I know people who have been in AA, OA, SA, and church Bible studies for years. It becomes a part of their life. It is an intricate, central point, like a foundation of rock. They know their group will love them and speak truth into their lives. And this is how small-group relationships become so powerful.

Isolation and loneliness are an epidemic in our society. So many people live lives of "quiet desperation," starving for intimate relationships. And this is why Mr. Hatch's story connects with all of us. Mr. Hatch worked the same drab job in a shoelace factory every day for years. For lunch, he had the same cheese-and-mustard sandwich with a peach for dessert. Everything was the same—day in, day out. He had no friends. He spoke to no one. He went to bed early. He went to the shoelace factory early every day. Then one day he came home from work and received a package from the mailman: a Valentine's Day box of candy with a card that simply said, "Somebody loves you."

Mr. Hatch's whole life changed because of this gesture of love. He started his day by speaking to the man at the newsstand when he purchased a newspaper. He began to bake brownies for his neighbors. His outlook on life changed because he had found out that somebody loved him. Then a few days later, the mailman returned to say that he had delivered the box to the wrong address. Mr. Hatch was devastated. He handed over the box with the ribbon attached.

Then the card. He watched the mailman deliver the box to the correct house, and then closed his door and proceeded back to his old life. He no longer spoke to the newspaper man or his neighbors. He isolated himself again. He withdrew. Everyone soon noticed that he had changed. They wondered what had happened and what had become of this outgoing, friendly man.

Soon the mailman told them of the mistake. The neighbors shook their heads and then decided to do something about it. One day Mr. Hatch came home from work and a huge banner hung over his apartment door, proclaiming, "Everybody loves you, Mr. Hatch!" He dabbed a tear with his handkerchief. He smiled again. He talked again. The man the neighbors had lost had returned.[1]

> # BODY
>
> Exercise can reduce the accumulation of body fat that accompanies aging and can slow, if not reverse, the substantial loss of muscle that usually goes hand in hand with the increase in body fat.

We live in a world where it is very difficult to be vulnerable, to be honest, to be who we really are because we fear that we will be rejected. So why bother with love? This was Mr. Hatch's theory until that mistaken package became a large banner. His experience summarizes small groups beautifully. A small group is the one place where we're loved and welcomed. They offer a place to take off our masks and let down our guards. They create a place to share all of our weaknesses and vulnerabilities. Then we are simply accepted. We are cared for. We are loved. Grace is extended. In small groups, we get to experience intimacy and authenticity. It's a safe place to say, "I stumbled this week. I am alone. I am scared, and I don't know what to do. I am broken and lost."

Knowing love, in the face of all my inadequacies, is life-changing. This is what we find in small groups. The journey to freedom will always lead me to a small group of people who will love me unconditionally. This is our hope. This is what we all long for—this experience of connection that we find in small groups. We need others to stay on the path to hope, health, and happiness.

REFLECTIONS

**SMALL GROUPS PROVIDE A SETTING WHERE I CAN BUILD
INTIMATE, SAFE RELATIONSHIPS THAT ENCOURAGE, SUPPORT,
AND HOLD ME ACCOUNTABLE ON MY JOURNEY OF CHANGE.**

- Do you have a small group with which you are connected that is supporting you and your efforts to change?

- What do you believe are the characteristics of a good small group? List four of these if you can.

EMOTIONS: CAN WE TRUST THEM?

Two prime ministers were sitting in a room discussing affairs of state, when suddenly a man burst through the door, shouting, stamping, and banging his fist on the desk. The resident prime minister admonished him: "Peter," he said, "kindly remember *Rule Number 6.*"

Amazingly, the man settled down, apologized, and left the room. The politicians returned to their conversation, only to be interrupted again twenty minutes later by a hysterical woman, slinging her arms and her hair and screaming about some incident that had happened in another meeting.

Again the prime minister spoke calmly: "Marie, please remember *Rule Number 6.*" Marie calmed down, apologized, and left the room.

When the scenario was repeated yet again, the other prime minister couldn't stand it any longer and said: "My dear friend, I've seen many things in my life, but nothing as remarkable as this. Would you be willing to share with me the secret of *Rule Number 6?*"

"It's very simple," replied the resident prime minister. "*Rule Number 6* is 'Don't take yourself and your situation so seriously.'"

"Ah," said the visiting prime minister, "that is a fine rule." Then, after a moment of pondering, he inquired, "And what, may I ask, are the other rules?"

The other prime minister replied, "There aren't any."[1]

Life is not a constant emergency. But when we live by our emotions, everything seems like an emotional emergency. This is especially true when we allow our emotions to make unwise judgments for us. Charles Dickens said, "There is nothing so strong or safe in an emergency of life as the simple truth." When emotions override our common sense, we do irrational things. This is called "emotional reasoning."[2] Sometimes we say, "Go with your gut," which has many parameters. But "going with our gut" doesn't mean that we should throw out our common sense. When we go with our emotions alone, we enter the realm of emotional reasoning.

The boss sends a memo saying she needs to meet with us, and we immediately believe we're in trouble, begin to worry, and let our emotions run wild. Or a coworker ignores us, and we wonder, *What did I do to him?* His insensitivity may actually be his own preoccupation over a spat he had with his wife before coming to work. There are numerous incidents in life where we go overboard emotionally and respond with erroneous feelings of fear and inadequacy.

Some of us attempt to defy our feelings altogether. For some of us, emotions become the enemy. But in our efforts to avoid pain, we actually cause more pain. Someone once said that we have to choose between feeling emotional pain and feeling nothing, they will choose to feel nothing. Processing our feelings and dealing with them in a positive, constructive way leads to growth. The route to normal emotions is to struggle through the painful ones. And one of the best tools available to combat emotional reasoning is an accountability partner. Others can see our blind spots and offer advice without being bound to the emotional emergency.

Accountability will be an integral part in helping us through emotional reasoning. Without accountability, many of us will not be able to sustain our efforts for change. We need accountability to develop the discipline of sticking with something, especially if it's new to us. All of us, at some point, struggle to have the endurance to finish the things we start. This is why built-in accountability will help us get through the tough spots. When we are tempted—and we will be tempted—having an accountability partner will make us think twice before succumbing to that temptation. We know we will have to answer to them for our actions. This helps us to avoid continuing our habits in secrecy, because secrecy breeds addiction and destructive habits.

Throughout our lives, we experience accountability. We are accountable to get to work on time or we may lose jobs. When I was a student athlete, I had to keep my grades up, attend class, and get to practice on time. I was accountable for all these things in order to be on the team.

In our day-to-day lives, accountability partners bring enormous relief to our problems. They become the one stable factor in our world. We have someone who will always be there for us to provide direction and support.

One cannot help but be moved by the story of the soldier who asked his officer if he might go out into the "no man's land" between the trenches in World War I to bring in one of his comrades who lay grievously wounded.

"You can go," said the officer, "but it's not worth it. Your friend has probably been killed, and you will throw your own life away."

The man went anyway. Somehow he managed to get to his friend, hoist him onto his shoulder, and bring him back to the trenches. The two of them tumbled in together.

The officer looked down tenderly on the would-be rescuer and said, "I told you it wouldn't be worth it. Your friend is dead, and now you are mortally wounded."

BODY

"Our tendency to have less-than-perfect program adherence is attributable to major obstacles. One is the daily battle we all wage with human nature. The other is the image of physical perfection that has become a cultural standard for the pursuit of health and fitness. Overcoming these obstacles is not easy, but understanding them is a big step toward developing motivation that will last a lifetime."

—Ruth McGinnis,
The Good Life

"It was worth it, though, sir," he said.

"How do you mean, 'worth it'? I tell you, your friend is dead!"

"Yes, sir," the boy answered, "but it was worth it, because when I got to him he was still alive, and he said to me, 'Jim, I knew you'd come.'"[3]

Everyone hopes for a friend like this. It's possible to find someone who will see us through to the end. We only have to seek them out.

Finding accountability is our responsibility. It's something we must ask for. Many people are confused about this aspect of accountability, but think about it: I'm not responsible for someone else unless they ask me to be. If you are involved in and committed to the process of change, seek out someone you trust and ask them to hold you accountable. I can't say to Bob, "Okay, Bob, I'm going to hold you accountable to change." If Bob doesn't want to change, then my suggestions are futile. Bob has to desire change for himself. True change takes intrinsic motivation. Sure, there will be a war going on inside us, where we waffle back and forth over whether or not we think we need accountability. This is normal. But it is not normal to think we can change in isolation. If you are committed to the process of change, seek out someone you trust and ask them to hold you accountable.

In Alcoholics Anonymous, they talk about the gift of recovery you receive. They have a saying that to keep recovery, you have to give it away. This is the other benefit of accountability. We will soon be an accountability partner for others. The greatest encouragement we can receive is when God starts using us in other people's lives. It gives us purpose in life. It helps us grow, as well.

There is a great scene in the movie, *As Good As It Gets*, where Melvin (Jack Nicholson) and Carol (Helen Hunt) are having dinner, and she tells him that she is going to leave the restaurant if he doesn't give her a compliment right then. So reluctantly and shyly, he tells her that being around her makes him want to be a better man. What a powerful compliment it was! Whenever we begin to have this type of influence on people, we experience the gift of recovery. We are giving back what we have received from others. And if you've ever wanted to have a positive influence in other people's lives, the way you do it is by respecting them. The apostle Peter said, "Show respect for all people: Love the brothers and sisters of God's family."[4] Respecting someone shows that you value him or her, and when you value people, they know it. They feel it. It makes them want to be the kind of person who respects and loves others, too.

AVOIDING PAIN ONLY CAUSES MORE PAIN

Emotions are real. They are a part of life, but they need not control us. This is why *Rule Number 6* can be successful. The quicker we get over being so serious about our emotions, the greater our chances of becoming whole—spirit, mind, and body. Team up with someone you trust for the next leg of your journey. We need accountability to help us learn to deal with and process our emotions.

REFLECTIONS

LIFE IS NOT A CONSTANT EMERGENCY. BUT WHEN WE LIVE BY OUR EMOTIONS, EVERYTHING SEEMS LIKE AN EMOTIONAL EMERGENCY.

- Have you ever made an emotional decision that you later regretted?

- Do you ever feel that your emotions are your enemy?

- How can an accountability partner help you sort through your emotions?

LIVING BY VISION AND NOT BY NEED

Dick Fosbury was the first high-jump competitor to use flop, starting in the 1960s. He went over head first with his back to the bar. Some people laughed. Others told him he'd never be able to perfect the move. The straddle method was the standard technique used in the high jump at that time, in which participants vaulted over the bar while facing it, with one arm and one leg leading. But Fosbury dared to modify the standard.

Fosbury said, "I was told over and over again that I would never be successful, that I was not going to be competitive and the technique was simply not going to work. All I could do was shrug and say, 'We'll just have to see.'" But Fosbury proved his skeptics wrong when he won the gold medal at the Mexico City Olympics in 1968. Today, his technique has become the standard in the high jump. It's known as the "Fosbury Flop."

Fosbury trained by vision, not by need. There's a huge difference. Vision asks new questions: *What if I jumped backwards? How can I invent a new standard?* The focus is different. When we live life out of a state of need, we ask desperate questions: *Will I make the jump? Will I qualify for the event?* Our inferiority complex overwhelms our ability to excel. We are in survival mode,

SPIRIT

"There is only one relationship that really matters, and that is your personal relationship to your personal Redeemer and Lord. If you maintain that at all cost, letting everything else go, God will fulfill his purpose for your life. One individual life may be of priceless value to God's purposes, and yours may be that life."

—OSWALD CHAMBERS, *MY UTMOST FOR HIS HIGHEST*

and some of us just give up after a few attempts. We surrender instead of tackling the situation courageously to discover a better way to jump higher. We accept the limits without trying to push them to a new level. But change is all about pushing ourselves to a new standard of living. Life doesn't have to be just average. Someone once said that success is a willingness to do what the average person is not willing to do. This is living by vision. But when we become preoccupied with our inferiorities, we inevitably get stuck. We focus on the shame of our mistake instead of learning from the failure and getting on with our lives. We think, *I should've been a better person*. And the way we accomplish our need to be better is by beating ourselves up, trying to use shame as a motivator for change.

Others live, not by addictions or relationships with people or things, but with a need to rearrange the past. We often become preoccupied with our failures and never get around to getting on with our lives. We live by the need to go back into the past to ruminate and mourn those failures, not to learn from them. We want to undo our mistakes, but this kind of thinking jeopardizes our future and will keep us in bondage.

Drowning in shame and trying to rearrange the past is not the way to move forward in life. It would be like a batter in baseball walking up to the plate and announcing to everyone that he now knows why he struck out the last time at bat. So, if they wouldn't mind, he'd like to go back and replay the third inning where he'd had a 3-2 count, so he can fix his mistake. This sounds crazy, but we do the same thing all the time. We go back in our minds and rehash old failures. We ruminate. We castigate ourselves. We see the solution we should have chosen and rake ourselves over the coals for not seeing it when it happened, whether it be ten years ago or two weeks ago. Life, much like baseball, doesn't work that way. A new inning is just that—a new inning, a new opportunity to hit a home run. When we live from an "I-need-to-be-better" standpoint, the moment our circumstances go wrong, we will plunge back to the depths of feeling eternally broken. We tell ourselves we really haven't changed. But what if, like Fosbury, we think of a new and different way to jump over our problems, a new way to motivate change?

When we live by vision, we don't look only to our past performances. Our focus is on what we *are* going to become, instead of what we *are not* going to become. This is why the apostle Paul said in the Bible, "I know that I have not yet reached that goal, but . . . there is one thing I always do. Forgetting the past and straining toward what is ahead, I keep trying to reach the goal and get the prize for which God called me through Christ to the life above."[1]

Michelangelo understood how to live a life driven by vision. When someone asked Michelangelo what he was doing as he chipped away at a block of stone, Michelangelo replied, "Can't you see there's an angel imprisoned in this block of stone? I'm working as hard as I can to set him free." He first had to envision the angel, and then with his focus on his vision, he worked to set the angel free. The apostle Paul did the same thing. He had to forget the past because there was nothing there to set him free. His goal was to chip the past away, so he could reach the new goal in the life above. This is why he also said, "If anyone belongs to Christ, there is a new creation. The old things have gone; everything is made new!"[2]

No longer can we use the old as a reference point for the future. It is gone! How can my old life tell my new life what it should be? Thinking about changing, we often say, "I'm not going to be *like that* anymore," but that is faulty thinking. When we make that statement, we're not defining what we should become. We're only saying we shouldn't be "like that."

Recovery is a matter of replacement. We replace the old life with a new one.

This doesn't mean that all our cravings magically go away. They won't; we will be tempted. We are not trying to put all of our energy into resisting, but into becoming someone different by replacing our addictions and longings with healthy patterns of living.

Recovery is learning new ways to do life. To set our spirits free, we need to chip away everything that's not associated with the fruit of the Spirit, which are "love, joy, peace, patience, kindness, goodness, faithfulness, gentleness, self-control."[3] We allow the Spirit's fruit to take shape in our lives and this replaces our unwanted behavior. One way to accomplish this transformation is to start with kindness, beginning to approach everything in life with kindness in mind. Then add another fruit of the Spirit, such as joy. Focus on joy until it becomes a natural response to life. Then proceed to the next fruit.

Wherever there is great vision, there is great passion. The word *passion* comes from the Latin word meaning "suffering." It has other connotations, such as sexual desire and zeal for a task. But I'm using it here in the context of suffering, which means we will *suffer* as we chip away the old life for the new. It will hurt us emotionally. But it also means that if we are temporarily lonely or hurting, we can suffer through it for a while because we know that we are going somewhere. We have a goal instead of being lonely and in pain without hope. Where there is hope, there is the vision needed to suffer through our current circumstances, to carve something hopeful and new out of our failure. Without vision, we suffer needlessly.

When I start living my life out of my vision, the vision ignites my purpose for living and drives my recovery. It's the power of the Spirit moving me along and controlling my future.

One of my favorite verses in Proverbs reads, "Where there is no vision, the people perish."[4] Living by vision is to set our eyes on what we want to become, and then we chip away everything that doesn't get us to our goal. Soon we will catch a glimpse of all that we can become, and the fulfillment of that replaces the emptiness and longing that we've been trying to fill with addictions and unhealthy relationships.

REFLECTIONS

THE KEY TO CHANGING AND GROWING IS TO BEGIN TO
LIVE OUT OF YOUR VISION, NOT YOUR NEED. WHEN I START
LIVING MY LIFE FROM MY VISION, THE VISION IGNITES MY
PASSION FOR LIVING AND DRIVES MY RECOVERY.

• How did Michelangelo envision the angel in the stone?

• What is your definition of the word *vision*?

• Do you have a vision for your life? If so, what is it?

PROGRESS, NOT PERFECTION

Jack began in the summer of 1995. Tired of being pudgy around the middle and suffering some painful gastrointestinal problems, he decided he needed to change. He wanted to lose some weight, but he never anticipated the change he would encounter. Overweight and not engaged in any physical exercise whatsoever, he began a strict low-fat diet and lost thirty-five pounds. Then, on a whim, he decided to begin shaping his body. At the time, his goals were modest. He just wanted to look in shape. Having lifted weights off and on since his teens, he decided to return to the YMCA. He'd maintained a membership for many years, but rarely used it. The surprising thing about his process of change was the way he enjoyed bodybuilding once he returned to the Y. He admits his initial lifts were pathetic. But they quickly increased to a level consistent with what they had been in the past.

Jack's decision to begin bodybuilding at the age of thirty-nine left him with what he calls a "considerable handicap." But despite his pudginess and age, he emerged from his recliner and his fast-food diet to discover the right combination of training, nutrition, and dedication, and it yielded impressive results. His body is now lean and fit.

Making progress in our plan of action will require that we show up, do our part, and trust God with the results. If we focus on progress and not perfection, it gives us the determination to stay the course. Most of the time, what

SPIRIT

"Pereverance is failing nineteen times and succeeding the twentieth."

—Julie Andrews

we can expect in recovery is two steps forward and one step back. We are a work in progress, not yet perfect.

There's a saying that *high expectations lead to low serenity, and low expectations lead to high serenity.* Apart from God, we can *try* to reform our behavior and *try* to white-knuckle our way through change, but when we do that, our focus is totally on our performance, not on progress.

Progress is a path of small transformations that take place each day. It's a path of brutal difficulty and sweet success. Plenty of mistakes litter the road of progress. Think about road construction. What a mess! All of those orange barrels, the congested traffic, the steamy blacktop, and the dump trucks hauling rock deep into the night. Road construction is not a pretty sight, but when it is finished, the traveling is smooth. Our vehicles glide over the pavement. But during the process, we get sick of seeing those men in orange vests. We want them to go away quickly, but they seem to hang around forever. Recovery is much like the construction on a highway. The progress is slow, and the rubble of barrels and loose rock is staggering. If we're not careful, we can take our eyes off the goal, become overwhelmed with the rubble around us, and quit.

This is what happened to the workers on the wall around Jerusalem. On Day 6, we discussed Nehemiah's rebuilding the wall around Jerusalem after their enemies had destroyed it. His first task was to survey the ruins, and he walked and wept around the broken-down wall. Then he assembled a team of people and began to build. Almost immediately, enemies rose up against the project. They attacked the builders' self-worth. They yelled to the workers, "What are those weak Jews doing? . . . If a fox climbed up on the stone wall they are building, it would break it down."[1] So, Nehemiah set guards around the wall as the people worked, attempting to silence the enemies' interference. They had dealt with the enemies without, but they still had to overcome the enemy within their hearts. When they reached the halfway point,[2] they looked around and said, "The workers are getting tired. There is so much trash we cannot rebuild the wall."[3] They were close to giving up.

Author Rick Warren says about this verse: "Some of you are discouraged because you are under tremendous pressure; your work load is unbelievable. God's message to you is *reorganize*. Reorganize your time; reorganize your schedule; refocus on your goal. Clear out the clutter and rubble and trivia, the things that are wasting your time. Then reorganize so that you work toward your main goal."[4]

MIND

"It is then the truest valor to dare to live."
—Sir Thomas Brown

THE BABY STEPS OF TRUE CHANGE

For most of us, our process of change will be marked by new beginnings. We will fail. We will get tired. Our strength will give out. Then we will start again, and we'll get better. This is how we transform. Change doesn't happen with one large step, but with multiple baby steps. It takes time. It's like hitting a golf ball. If I've always hit at a golf ball with some very bad habits in my swing, then it's going to take time for the new habits to replace the old ones. Because some old habits have been in our lives for a long time, perhaps even our whole life, we have to keep a realistic expectation of what it will take to change those habits.

God doesn't expect perfection. What He expects is humility. He wants us to work with Him and work with the people He has put in our life to help make progress a reality.

In his book, *Addictions and Grace*, Dr. Gerald May says that our addictions divide our will, splitting it right down the middle.[5] A part of us sincerely wants to change, but there's another part, just as strong, that wants to hold on to our addictions or destructive patterns. This is why it is crucial to surround ourselves with accountability partners and a small group. This is where sane voices instruct and encourage us to get back on our feet.

Determination and perseverance are wonderful. We need courage in order to succeed. But mostly, we need to be aware of our progress over time. It will happen if we just keep showing up and working on it.

INTRINSIC VERSUS EXTRINSIC MOTIVATION

Some of us get extrinsically motivated to change, and think, *I'm going to lose my driver's license if I don't stop drinking,* or, *My wife is going to leave me if I don't stop looking at pornography.* Extrinsic negative consequences will motivate us, but they fail to sustain change over the long haul, because when we get back those things we've lost (i.e., driver's licenses), we will lose the extrinsic motivation, and the tendency to fall back into the old lifestyle becomes natural. Motivation has to be sustained, and we do this by being *intrinsically* motivated.

When someone is intrinsically motivated, it's not about making anyone happy or trying to avoid a consequence. It's an internal desire to work together with God from a perspective of *I want to be different.* We focus on who we are becoming. We commit to be in it for the long haul. We are going to give ourselves the time, the grace, and the permission to work through our mistakes. This is recovery. It's not about perfection. It's about progress.

Keep showing up and walking with God. Reorganize your priorities. Align yourself with extrinsic motivation if you have to, but realize that true change is intrinsic and lasting.

REFLECTIONS

MAKING PROGRESS IN OUR PLAN OF ACTION WILL REQUIRE THAT
WE SHOW UP, DO OUR PART, AND TRUST GOD WITH THE RESULTS.
IF WE FOCUS ON PROGRESS AND NOT PERFECTION, IT GIVES US
THE DETERMINATION WE NEED TO STAY THE COURSE.

- Do you feel a compulsion to be perfect?

- What do you think is driving your need for perfection?

- If you could ask God to help you with one area of your life, what would it be?

GIVING YOURSELF PERMISSION
TO START AGAIN

In Day 28, I noted how John kept a membership at the YMCA, but initially rarely used it. This is quite common. Many people start a workout program, but few actually maintain it. The key to success is to give ourselves permission to restart our programs the way John did. This is a vital part of the process of change.

Let's say we are working out at the YMCA three days a week, but one week we miss a few days. Maybe we are sick or work takes us out of town. Then the following week other things come up, and before we know it, four weeks have gone by, and we haven't worked out at all. Now we're inactive again, and the inner critic begins to berate us for failing. But we're only failures if we *stay* inactive. Quitting is the only failure. John chose not to be a failure. Sure, he was inactive for many years, but he got back in the gym anyway. He reentered the process of change.

In his book, *A Gentle Path through the Twelve Steps*, Dr. Patrick Carnes asks the question, "Why is recovery so hard?"[1] He believes one answer to this question is that recovery or change is about reclaiming integrity. It's about respecting ourselves enough to do the hard work of change. Sure, it's easier to be a couch potato than hit the gym three days a week. But laziness leads to a lack of self-respect, and it's hard to change if we don't respect ourselves enough to do so. Recovering from an inactive lifestyle means that we will have to reclaim integrity, and reclaiming integrity is about self-respect.

First, having self-respect begins when we accept ourselves. When we accept ourselves, we understand that we may have to work on our faults. And we will need all the strength we can muster to do it, because hating ourselves ties one arm behind our back. Charles Reynolds Brown, dean of Yale Divinity School (1911–1928), once said, "Everyone is born into the world with a certain unrealized capacity. Let him accept his hand as it was dealt to him, and play the game, without wasting his time bemoaning the fact that his cards are not all aces and faces. Accept yourself for what you are, and for what, by the grace of God, you may yet become, and play the game."[2]

The Bible says that all of us should set aside everything that hinders and run the race that is set before us.[3] No one gets to choose his or her race. We don't get the opportunity to choose between being perfect and being imperfect. All of us are imperfect, and we'll remain that way until we die. The key is to "set aside" the things that are keeping us inactive in the process of change, such as laziness, self-defeating addictions, and listening to the inner critic that tells us we will never change. These are the things we've been discussing throughout the book, and these can't be defeated if we are divided against ourselves. We have to accept ourselves for who we are, and then work to become who, by the grace of God, He wants us to be. As the Serenity Prayer says, "God grant me the serenity to accept the things I cannot change, the courage to change the things I can, and wisdom to know the difference." This is a model prayer for self-acceptance.

Second, having self-respect means being ourselves in every situation. Charles Reynolds Brown wrote, "Some people are hypocrites because they try to appear much better than they really are. Other people are hypocrites because, for some reason, they are afraid to allow that which is true and fine in them to be

> ## MIND
>
> "In the confrontation between the stream and the rock, the stream always wins— not through strength but by perseverance."
> —H. JACKSON BROWN, JR.

BODY

Citing a study of 10,000 women aged 40 to 55, Miriam Nelson of Tufts University noted that 8 percent had difficulty doing simple physical tasks, such as climbing a flight of stairs, walking around a city block, or carrying a grocery bag. Frailty is going to catch up with these people in their 50s instead of their 80s or 90s. This is an epidemic of weakness that is especially occurring among American women and is also happening in men, as well. Boy, do we need strength training.

revealed."[4] The journey to freedom includes learning to be honest with ourselves. We stand in our own shoes. We speak from our own heart. We become true to ourselves and God. When we slip up, we get back up and continue our courageous battle to become true to ourselves.

Third, having self-respect means living a life of humility. We understand and accept our limitations, the way Muhammad Ali did as he was about to take off on an airplane flight. The stewardess reminded Ali, who was in his prime at the time, to fasten his seatbelt. He shot back brashly, "Superman don't need no seatbelt." The stewardess quickly replied, "Yeah, and Superman don't need no airplane, either." Ali humbly fastened his seatbelt.

Understanding our limitations means that we realize that we're not Superman or Superwoman. We can't change our lives without God's help. This is true humility, as we've been learning. But sometimes we only accept God's help in certain areas of our lives. When we need help staying sober, we don't mind asking God for help. But we fail to depend on Him in our marriage or to help us become a better parent or to help us financially. We pick and choose areas where we allow God to help. But to get the type of life transformation that we need, we have to give God everything. We must come to the realization that change must happen at the core of who we are. This allows God to execute a plan of change by His strength. We do this by entering the process of transformation in our entire lives, instead of only in certain areas of our lives.

Think about washing a car. You would never wash only the hood of the car, leaving the remaining parts dirty, would you? When you wash a car, you most likely complete the job by submitting the entire body of the car to the process.

You don't choose the parts of the body that only the driver can see, such as the hood, and then deceive yourself into thinking that by washing only one area of the car that somehow you've made the entire car clean. It's the same when we submit our lives to God. Allowing Him to get us sober and keep us sober is only one area. To have a life of freedom, we have to subject all areas to God's help.

Fourth, gaining self-respect is a result of setting goals and achieving them. We feel good about ourselves when we achieve goals. So, we should set some goals. Make them easy in the beginning. If you fail, start again. Get back up. If you need to lose weight, then set a goal to lose a pound a week and take the steps to achieve it. Work out. Walk. Swim. Do some type of activity. If you need to stop an addiction, then attend a twelve-step program once a week. This is a start, and sometimes all we need to get us going again is to take the first step. Give yourself permission to get back in the race.

There was once a man who knew how to restart after failure. When he was seven years old, his family was forced out of his home on a legal technicality, and he had to work to help support them. At age nine, his mother died. At twenty-two, he lost his job as a store clerk. He wanted to go to law school, but his education was lacking. At twenty-three, he went into debt to become a partner in a small store. At twenty-six, his business partner died, leaving him a huge debt that took him many years to repay. At twenty-eight, he asked his girlfriend of four years to marry him. She said no. At thirty-seven, on his third try, he was elected to Congress, but two years later, he failed to be reelected. At forty-one, his four-year-old son died. At forty-five, he ran for the Senate and lost. At forty-seven, he failed as the vice-presidential candidate. At forty-nine, he ran for the Senate again and lost. At fifty-one, he was elected the president of the United States. His name was Abraham Lincoln, a man whom many consider our greatest leader.

The one thing that remained constant throughout Lincoln's life was the way he restarted after failure. He got back up. He set goals—he achieved some of them and failed at others. But he respected his ability enough to restart time and time again.

Self-respect begins when we accept ourselves with humility and truly become ourselves in every situation. We set goals and achieve them. We become something different and something better. If we slip up, we learn from it and move forward. The journey to freedom requires consistency and a willingness to run the race that is set before us, even if, like Abraham Lincoln's, the race is littered with hurdles and past defeat.

REFLECTIONS

ACCEPT YOURSELF FOR WHO YOU ARE, AND FOR WHO, BY THE GRACE OF GOD, YOU MAY YET BECOME.

- When you fail, how long does it take for you to rebound and get started again?

- Pretend you failed at a task. What would you say to yourself about this failure?

- Do you extend compassion and patience to yourself in all situations?

DESIRE TO BE SET FREE

In the movie *It's a Wonderful Life*, George Bailey longs to be successful and travel the world. He believes that monetary success will make him happy and content, and this becomes his goal and his passion. But through a chain of events, he never leaves Bedford Falls. He settles down, marries, and has what he believes is a mediocre career. He has friends and success, but not the type of success he'd envisioned. He feels stuck in the small-town mode, away from the bright lights and the big city. Other friends have gone on to make lots of money and have accomplished great things, but George remained in Bedford Falls. Why? George had originally been headed off to college when his father died, leaving him to run the family business.

George is the faithful one that keeps the Bailey Savings and Loan afloat so others can have affordable housing. Then enters the evil Mr. Potter, who is trying to buy the Savings and Loan and turn Bedford Falls into Pottersville. He steals money from George's absent-minded uncle, and it looks as if George may have to go to jail. Everything falls apart, and he ends up on a bridge on Christmas Eve, ready to commit suicide. Then Clarence, George's guardian angel, takes him on a journey to look back at his life. George gets to see what life would have been like if he'd never been born. When he comes to the end of this journey with Clarence, we see him standing on the bridge looking down, saying, "Please, God, I want to live again." At the end of the movie, the people of Bedford Falls make a toast to George, "To the richest man in town!" This is how George Bailey discovers that true freedom is not found in money or status.

It's a Wonderful Life provides a great example of someone living in a self-made prison, because George doesn't have an addiction. He's not an alcoholic or dependent on any physical substances. But his internal life is dominated and controlled by an obsession to make money and see the world—to be different from his father. His happiness rests upon this fallacy to the point that he almost ends his life because of it.

We can become dependent on relationships, money, success, beauty, or fame—all because we are trying so hard not to feel lonely, poor, ugly, purposeless, or unsuccessful. This is why God warns us throughout the Bible to guard our hearts against false idols. False idols can take the place of having an open relationship with Him, and becoming dependent on anything other than God builds a self-made prison. It's like being dependent on drugs or alcohol. Just as these substances put us in bondage, so does an all-out blitz to focus life on self and the acquisition of material possessions. As George Bailey discovered, money and status can never fully satisfy.

I've dealt with numerous George Bailey types at Restore—men and women who've become disillusioned with life. They came to Restore feeling like failures because they have failed to achieve their dreams, even though they were very successful by other standards. They had nice families and good friends, but they deceived themselves into believing that just because they hadn't reached a certain level of income that they were failures. They believed life had cheated them or passed them by, only to bless friends or neighbors with riches, beauty, fame, and good fortune. So, they had become bitter.

It's impossible to embrace and fully live in the present as long as we are trying to derive happiness from something outside of a relationship with God. It has always been God's desire that Christ's mission be one to set us free by turning

SPIRIT

"I believe that God's basic nature is love. I don't think that we can even fathom the depth of what that really means. If love were like a substance that you could hold, that's what God would be."

–MIKE S. O'NEIL,
THE POWER TO CHOOSE

our hearts to Him, instead of to materialism, addictions, or being dependent on the approval of others. But it's hard to walk away from a life focused on self. We keep holding on because we are afraid of what will take its place. The path of least resistance is to hold on to what we have, even if it never sets our hearts free.

We want all the benefits of the good life, and we set ourselves up for disappointment because many of us never achieve all of these things. We start our adult lives by saying something like, "I will be a millionaire by the time I'm thirty years old." And if we miss the mark, even though we have rich and endearing relationships and a comfortable lifestyle, we still feel like failures and become dissatisfied and bitter.

Sometimes it's easier to keep asking the question, *Why haven't I received riches and power?* than it is to move beyond it. Often, there is no logical answer to our questions. God has His reasons, but sometimes He doesn't choose to share them with us. This can be tough to deal with, but there is no easy answer other than to keep moving. Don't become bitter. Keep persevering. There's nothing wrong with having strong goals and a sense of ambition, but it is wrong to base our happiness on it. This is why Christ said, "If anyone would come after me, he must deny himself and take up his cross daily and follow me. For whoever wants to save his life will lose it, but whoever loses his life for me will save it."[1] Think about this when you feel trapped and bitter. Perhaps you are depending on all the wrong things to make you happy and fulfilled.

REFLECTIONS

FOR MANY PEOPLE, HAPPINESS IS CONTINGENT UPON MONEY, PRESTIGE, SUCCESS, OR RELATIONSHIPS.

- Have you ever had the compulsion to be successful? Why or why not? Were your reasons the right reasons?

- It's impossible to embrace and fully live in the present as long as we are trying to derive happiness from something outside of a relationship with God. So, is there anything you are holding on to from the past or even concerning the future that is keeping you from fully embracing the present?

FINISH STRONG

GRIEVING THE PAST SO YOU CAN REACH FOR THE FUTURE

One of my favorite *Twilight Zone* episodes is about someone who is trying to relive the past. A middle-aged businessman is working in a large metropolitan city. It's a dog-eat-dog atmosphere, and he's fighting to stay alive in the brutal competition. One day he gets into his car and aimlessly begins to drive. When he comes upon a small town, he parks his car, gets out, and starts walking. As he's walking, he is shocked to realize that he's traveled back in time to his childhood. His old neighborhood is exactly as it was when he was a ten-year-old boy. And the weird *Twilight* Zone twist is that he runs into himself as a boy and calls out to himself. But the boy never hears him. Then he goes to his childhood home and tries to tell his father who he is and that he has traveled back in time, and they have a very moving conversation about how he wishes he could relive his childhood.

The story resonates with me because I know how this man feels. I, too, struggle with wanting to relive my youth. There is a powerful line in an old Christmas song that says, "Toyland, Toyland, little girl and boy land, but once you pass its borders you can never return again." But what this song doesn't tell us is that getting beyond the borders of our childhood may not happen with some people until well into adulthood. Sometimes actual chronological age

MIND

"Fill your mind with the thought that God is there. And once your mind is truly filled with that thought, when you experience difficulties, it will be as easy as breathing for you to remember, 'My heavenly Father knows all about this!'"

—OSWALD CHAMBERS,
*MY UTMOST FOR
HIS HIGHEST*

has nothing to do with it. The *Twilight Zone* episode touches on this truth. Stan also experienced a similar breakthrough when he came to visit me at Restore.

Sixty-year-old Stan told me everything over the course of an afternoon. He was on his fifth step in the twelve-step program, the step in which you sit down with one person and share your life story. It's called a "personal inventory." The goal is to attempt to answer these types of questions: *Why do I drink? Why do I seek out pornography? Why do I feel rage? Why do I have such a negative self-image? Why am I the way I am?*

So, I was listening to Stan's story about how he grew up with an alcoholic father. He told me about how he so desperately desired his father's love, but his father never expressed affection. Instead, he was mean and prone to fits of rage. One evening when Stan was ten years old, he felt an overwhelming compulsion to go put his arms around his father and tell him how much he loved him. He mustered up the courage, went to his father, put his arms around him, and said, "Dad, I love you." His father pushed him away and said, "What's up with you? Leave me alone." So, Stan never tried again.

Because of his relationship with his father, Stan felt insignificant and unworthy of love his whole life. As he told his story, it became evident that I was not talking to a sixty-year-old man, but a ten-year-old boy who was still longing for his father's love and yet was still feeling unworthy of it.

We need to rescue our hearts from the past. The way we do this is by expressing grief. We work through the grief by feeling the pain. In their book *God Will Make a Way,* Cloud and Townsend write, "Our past losses and hurts can be healed as we allow ourselves to attach to them the sadness that's warranted. Simply put, we need to *grieve.* It's a critical step in God's process for healing hurt."[1] Letting go to reach for the future means we must stop trying to relive the past. Sometimes we relive the past because it was safe back then. It was joyful and carefree, with no responsibilities or problems.

For twenty-five years, I had the same recurring dream. In my dream, I'm in junior-high school, the most joyful period of my life. I'm a young teenager riding bikes with my friends, free to roam wherever, to play games and laugh. No huge responsibilities. A time of innocence and play. I had all these great dreams of what I was going to do with my life, about what I was going to be. Everything seemed plausible. Most of my life was still ahead of me. But in my dream, I'm walking around the school checking doors, peeping through the windows into the gym, wanting so much to get inside, but the doors are locked. I would wake up from the dream and feel an incredible sense of sadness and longing.

We usually think of experiencing a loss as when someone dies, but the loss of dreams can also trigger a time of mourning. Longing and thirsting to go back, just like the man in the *Twilight Zone* episode, I wanted to find that twelve-year-old boy so I could tell him not to waste his life. I guess it was because I felt I had so much hope back then. No failures to speak of. But as I became an adult, my addictions and divorce left me fragile. Maybe these experiences left me longing for a more innocent time.

I never dealt with my grief until I entered a grief-counseling class to be certified to help families at the YMCA. In this class, I found myself working through my own grief, and this is when I realized just how much I'd lost back then. But then I realized that at the end of lost hopes and dreams is Christ. That's the good news. The good news is that He gives new beginnings. We may not be able to relive the past, but we can begin again as we grieve the past and let it go. This is why I don't have that dream anymore. The Lord has given me a new dream, a new vision, and a new purpose.

A friend once told me that early in our lives we only know how to *get* things—but we don't learn how to *let go*. As we move through our journey to freedom, many of us are going to need to look into our lives and move through the process of grief as we let go and complete the losses of our lives. Then we will be able to dream new dreams and begin to embrace the wonderful gift of Christ's promise, "With God all things are possible."[2]

In an earlier chapter, I mentioned the phrase "the darkness of the beginning." In our darkest moment, the most important decision we will make is to reach out for the future. The best part of life can start now. The new beginning will grow from the fertile ashes of past destruction. In this soil, God's power is made possible because we realize our strength is ashes and only God has the ability to take our past destruction and use it for good. There's a great verse in the Bible that says, "We know that in everything God works for the good of those who love him."[3]

The journey to freedom is about new beginnings. So, wherever you are, whatever your age, wherever you've been, the best part of your life begins now. It did for Stan. He grieved and moved beyond the borders of his sad childhood. I grieved the loss of my joyful childhood and embraced a new adulthood. So, this final week is about taking the journey. Reach out and make these last days count. Let this encouragement propel you along in the process of change.

REFLECTIONS

WE NEED TO RESCUE OUR HEARTS FROM THE PAST. WE NEED TO GRIEVE KEY LOSSES SO SOMETHING NEW CAN BEGIN IN OUR LIVES.

- Are there different types of loss outside of loss caused by death?

- Have you had a loss in your life that you feel you need to grieve in order to be able to move forward?

- How do you usually grieve a loss? How might you need to change?

TAKE A RISK:
STEP OUT OF THE BOAT

It was sometime after midnight when Jesus sent His disciples across the lake. Jesus needed alone time with the Father. Reluctant to leave Him, the disciples pushed their boats into the water. Later, a storm began to brew in the far corner of the lake. Then the light storm became a squall. The wind flapped the sails. The choppy water smacked the hull. And then, a strange thing happened. It seemed as if there was a ghost approaching them, walking on the water. As Christ approached the boat, He could see their frightened stances. But Christ said, "Have courage! It is I. Do not be afraid."[1]

Most of us would have been relieved and invited Him into the boat. But Peter, the adventurous one, wanted to walk on the water, too. He called to Christ, "LORD, if it is really you, then command me to come to you on the water." Christ said, "Come."[2] So, Peter stepped out.

The riskiest step of any new venture is always the first step. It's the bravest, too. Take Peter, for example. Our logic and understanding of the scientific rules of this world tell us that we can't walk on water. Because a human weighs more than water, it is a scientific fact that the human will sink. Simple, right? But sometimes we have to defy our logic and understanding. So, why don't we take that first risky step to change? Often, it's because we don't want to let go of the familiar. Change breaks the rules; something different happens. This fear is what keeps us in the boat, where we are comfortable.

To change anything in our lives, risk will be involved. Changing deeply ingrained habits, destructive patterns, and addictions requires great risk. Every day we are involved in activities of risk. Consider these facts:

- Automobiles cause 20 percent of all fatalities.
- Trains, planes, and boats cause 16 percent of accidents.
- Walking near roads and highways causes 15 percent of all accidents.
- Household accidents make up 17 percent of all accidents.[3]

> ## SPIRIT
>
> "It is within my power either to serve God or not to serve Him. Serving Him, I add to my own good in the good of the whole world. Not serving Him, I forfeit my own good and deprive the world of that good which was in my power to create."
>
> —Leo Tolstoy

If we attempted to stay away from these areas, we would not travel at all; it would be too risky. But each day we push out into a world of the unknown, where anything can happen.

The first step is always the hardest. Notice that Peter stepped *toward* Christ. Peter needed Christ's power and His strength. Courage empowers us as we trust the One toward whom we are stepping. The courage for our first step will come from moving toward Christ, as well. We need His power and grace to do for us what we cannot do for ourselves. What is impossible for you or me alone is possible with Christ, for all things are possible with Him. When Jesus said, "Come," Peter believed and walked toward Christ.

Second, Peter made the mistake of taking his focus off of Christ. He allowed the storm to distract him. Likewise, we often take our eyes off of the solution in front of us and concentrate on the negative circumstances. We begin to believe that we can't overcome, and we begin to sink. But notice that Peter did a key thing. When he started to sink, he took Christ's hand.

Many times we're like the young boy who was doing his best to lift a rock that was too large for someone his size. He grunted and puffed as he tried various methods for lifting the rock. But in spite of all of his efforts, the rock wouldn't budge. His father walked by, and after watching his son's struggle for a few moments, asked if he was having trouble. The boy answered, "Yes, I've tried everything, and it won't move." The father replied, "Are you sure you have tried every possibility, that you have used every resource at your disposal?" The boy looked up with frustration and exhaustion filling his face and grunted out a "Yes!" With kindness, the father bent over and softly said, "No, my son, you haven't. You haven't asked for my help."

Many times, we try lifting things that are too heavy for us. We exhaust our strength. We become frustrated and defeated when all we had to do was ask for Christ's help. He reaches out through people, groups, or a team at work, and all we have to do is grab His hand. If you try to stand alone, you will sink.

Peter had an incredible experience with Christ when he walked on the water. All day, every day, we have opportunities to experience Christ, to step out and trust Him. We only need to build into our schedule appointed times to meet with Him.

One of Rabbi Ben Jochai's pupils once asked why God hadn't furnished the children of Israel enough manna in the desert to last for a full year. The rabbi used a parable to supply the answer. He said, "Once there was a king who had a son to whom he gave a yearly allowance, paying him the entire sum on a fixed date. It soon happened that the day on which the allowance was due was the only day of the year when the father ever saw his son. So, the king changed his plan and gave his son day-by-day that which was sufficient for the day; then the son visited his father every morning. How he needed his father's unbroken love, companionship, wisdom, and giving!"[4]

Our journey to freedom begins when we accept the risk and take the first step. We remain focused, but if we slip, we grab His hand. Storms will occur. Old feelings of remorse, low self-esteem, and doubt will cause distractions, but remember the One who is in the storm with you. Reach out and take His hand.

REFLECTIONS

TO CHANGE ANYTHING IN OUR LIVES, RISK WILL BE INVOLVED.

- Can you tell of a time when you took a risk? What happened?

- Are there different levels of risk? Are there high risks and low risks? What makes them different? Which one is harder to take?

- In what "boat" are you sitting today that you need to get out of in order to change?

PERSEVERANCE: THE STRENGTH TO FINISH THE RACE

Thomas Edison gave us—among countless other things—some wise thoughts regarding perseverance. The famous inventor made thousands of trial runs and prototypes before he finally got the light bulb to operate. One day, a workman to whom he'd given a task said, "Mr. Edison, it cannot be done."

Edison said, "How often have you tried?"

"About two thousand times."

"Go back and try two thousand more; you have only found that there are two thousand ways in which it cannot be done."

Edison also said, "Genius is one-percent inspiration and ninety-nine-percent perspiration."[1]

Most of us have an aversion to any type of pain or discomfort. We try a few times to change, then we give up when it doesn't seem to work. We live in this "microwave generation" where we want everything fixed *right now*. We believe discomfort is a sin.

One of the most confusing statements in the Bible says, "My brethren, count it all joy when you fall into various trials, knowing that the testing of your faith produces patience."[2] We don't think about having joy in a trial. We think, *How can I get out of this painful predicament?* No one says, "Where can I find a trial today? I want to test my faith."

God is not sadistic, nor does He think we should be sadistic people and go about punishing ourselves. He desires growth in our soul, and He knows that sticking with the pain and discomfort of some of our circumstances teaches us patience. We learn to endure because it leads to a place of victory.

I remember how much I hated summer practice as a high-school and college football player. We were out in the 90-degree weather twice a day. Sweat poured from every pore in our bodies. When someone tackled us and plowed us into the ground, sweat flew off us like throwing a soaked sponge at a wall. No one enjoyed practice season. We wanted to get to the games. We wanted to play an opponent under the bright lights of the stadium. We knew if we could endure practice and weight training, we'd get the incredible reward of playing in a game. Plus when we got to the game, we discovered that all of the practicing gave us the strength and confidence to be successful. Later on, I realized how much the game of football taught me about life.

Life is much like an athletic event or a race. Life requires perseverance to see it through, especially when we are trying to change bad habits or addictions. So count it as joy when you have to face down an addiction every day, because the victory over the addiction is shaping your soul one small step at a time. Anyone who wins the battle of weight management can tell you it came off one pound at a time. We accomplish any goal by persevering through small steps. Think of Dave Ramsey, the financial guru. At one time, he went bankrupt. Now he's a best-selling author, telling others how to manage their finances. Ask him how he did it, and he'll tell you it was through perseverance. He attacked one bill at a time until he got it paid. Then he did the same thing with the next one.

Passion comes from purpose. In his book, *The Power of Purpose,* Richard Leider writes, "Purpose is the conscious choice of what, where, and how to

BODY

"Some of the benefits of strength training include replacing fat with muscle, which in turn increases strength and energy, as well as improving balance and flexibility and boosts metabolism, a key to permanent weight loss by as much as 15 percent. Strength training also has had an impact on numerous medical conditions; it strengthens the heart, relieves arthritis symptoms, lifts depression, and prevents or reverses the bone loss commonly known as osteoporosis."

—Miriam Nelson

make a positive contribution to our world. It is the theme, quality, or passion we choose to center our lives around. Once we discover our gifts and what moves us, the whole world takes on a new energy. Our life becomes a thing of spiritual significance."[3] This is why it's important to find our purpose in the world. Our life needs a theme and a reason, and once we discover that, it will be the force behind perseverance. Without passion, life becomes drudgery.

Patience is the main ingredient for perseverance. The Bible says, "But let patience have its perfect work, that you may be perfect and complete, lacking nothing."[4] Anything worth achieving, any struggle or challenge, requires patience. We don't plant a garden, and then expect a crop overnight. We give the invisible time to become visible. The Bible says, "A farmer patiently waits for his valuable crop to grow from the earth and for it to receive the autumn and spring rains. You, too, must be patient. Do not give up hope . . ."[5]

We can plant healthy habits, but we must not expect instant results. Persevere with patience, knowing that in due time your new healthy habits will produce a crop of rewards. Addictions become easier to resist. The pounds will come off. Destructive patterns lose their grip. But it won't happen unless we are patient. Another verse in the Bible sates, ". . . we also glory in tribulations, knowing that tribulation produces perseverance; and perseverance, character; and character, hope" (Rom. 5:3–4 NKJV).

It's a natural progression.

In a *Sports Illustrated* article, Francie Larrieu Smith, who at the age of thirty-nine competed in her fifth Olympic event as a marathon hopeful, once said about a race, "[T]hat's what gives me the old hope, if I can see the finish line I can always find something."[6]

When everything in us says to just lie down and quit, we can draw from God the strength to finish. To persevere, let patience have time to work. The Bible says, "And let us not grow weary while doing good, for in due season we shall reap if we do not lose heart."[7]

REFLECTIONS

ANY TIME WE TRY TO CHANGE SOMETHING, WE CAN EXPECT SOME LEVEL OF DISCOMFORT.

• Do you believe that persevering through trials and tribulations develops strong character? Explain.

• Is patience the main ingredient of perseverance?

• Are you patient with yourself, or do you give up too quickly?

THE STRUGGLE FOR FREEDOM

A reporter once asked advice columnist Ann Landers what question she received the most. In response, Ann said that the most common question she receives is, *What's wrong with me?*

We hear this question on a continual basis at Restore. People feel broken, have little hope things will change, and just want to know what's wrong with them. This is why it's essential for those in recovery or healing to hear the voice of Christ speaking through the ages, "Come to me, all of you who are tired and have heavy loads, and I will give you rest."[1] And we should go to Him. Just as we are. We should go, fully aware of what little we have to offer and knowing that His love will drive out the fears caused by our addictions and destructive habits.

People who come to Restore usually aren't seeking God. They want to change and improve their lifestyle, their health, and their relationships. They want the pain to stop. But soon they discover that theirs is not only a physical or emotional dilemma, but also a spiritual dilemma. When they realize this, then they are ready to hear God calling them to a place of safety where they can lay their burdens down. Their problem leads them to God. It's much like what bees go through to ensure the healthy development of their young. The queen lays each egg in a six-sided cell filled with enough pollen and honey to feed the egg until it reaches a certain stage of maturity. Then the

queen bee seals the capsule with wax. When the occu-
pant exhausts its supply of nourishment, the tiny crea-
ture emerges from its confinements. But it wrestles,
tussles, and strains to get through the wax seal. And in
the agony of its exit, the bee rubs off the membrane that
encases its wings—so that when it does emerge, it is
able to fly.

When I hit bottom, I wanted God to take the pain
away. Then I understood God's invitation and slowly I
began to turn homeward toward Him. I realized my
journey was no longer about stopping the pain or having a better life, even though it ended up being a new
life. I discovered that an incredibly loving God had captured my heart. He transformed my desires and every
aspect of my life by loving me, guiding me, comforting
me, nurturing me, encouraging me, and supporting
me. I came to a place where my burdens fell away and I entered into a loving
relationship with Him.

HOW TO LOVE GOD IN RETURN

We know that relationships aren't one-sided. If they were, they wouldn't last
long. So, the part we play in a relationship with God is much like a marriage.
In a marriage relationship, we should live for what's best for the relationship.
Therefore, we do our best to not become involved in behavior that damages
that mutual love and understanding. If we have ongoing affairs in our marriage, then the relationship will shatter. No one wants to stay married to
someone who can't be faithful. And this is what God wants from us. He
desires faithfulness.

Once we begin a relationship with God, it should not be a relationship based
on God's wrath or on our fear of Him. The Bible says, "Where God's love is,
there is no fear, because God's perfect love drives out fear. It is punishment that

makes a person fear, so love is not made perfect in the person who fears."[2]

Many times, I've fled out of fear and searched for something that offered safety. I thought my addictions provided safety, but they only put me in further bondage and fear. This is so typical. Most of the time, we never realize that our addictions and dependencies only deepen our fear. In this bondage, we feel as though God would never want a relationship with us. We feel tainted and end up wandering for many years through our lives searching for love.

Dr. Gerald May writes, "For the power of addiction to be overcome, human will must act in concert with divine will. The human spirit must flow with the Holy Spirit. Personal power must be aligned with the power of grace. . . . The alignment of our will with God's must happen at a heart level, through authentic choices of faith that are empowered by God."[3] We can't defeat addiction on our own, nor can we turn everything over to God and expect Him to do all the work for us. We must still choose an authentic faith and trust Him with all of our hearts, taking one step at a time. My efforts to change are no longer about just using God to get what I want, but something much deeper. I dedicate and devote everything in my life to a loving relationship with God, and everything flows from this central relationship.

I will definitely struggle through the pain at first. But as I do, the pain does something to my soul. I am being transformed.

BODY

"Last but not least, it is essential to have a measure of anticipation and joy for whatever exercise or activity you choose to take on. Your physical exrtion needs to delight you in some way, or it simply will not become a consistent part of your life."
—RUTH McGINNIS, THE GOOD LIFE

REFLECTIONS

A SPIRITUAL DILEMMA IS JUST AS REAL AS PHYSICAL AND EMOTIONAL TURMOIL.

• What are your reflections on the process of the bee in this chapter?

• Do you believe a relationship with God should be two-sided, where we give back as much love as we receive? Why or why not?

BLUEPRINT TO FREEDOM: DESIGNING YOUR PERSONAL PLAN OF CHANGE

Today you will design a Personal Plan of Change. You will set goals in the three areas of change we've discussed—spirit, mind, and body. After defining these goals, you will write out the steps it will take to achieve these goals. Finally, you will put together your "Freedom Team," which consists of the key people who will walk with you along the journey to freedom. They will provide direction, support, encouragement, inspiration, and accountability to help you accomplish your plan of action.

Step 1—Write out your goals in the space provided below. For example, if you desire a closer walk with God, then write this in the *Spirit* category below. If you want to learn how to renew your mind by not allowing the inner critic to control you, then write that in the *Mind* category. If you want to lose weight, write that in the *Body* category.

- *Spirit*

- *Mind*

- *Body*

Step 2—Take specific steps to meet your goals:
  - *Spirit*
    Example: attend church regularly; begin a twelve-step program; spend ten minutes a day in prayer

- *Mind*

  Example: begin a twelve-step program; contact a therapist

- *Body*

  Example: walk thirty minutes daily; increase fruits and vegetables in my diet; decrease sweets and fats; lift weights three times a week

Step 3—Find a support team:
- Find a support community.

  (Choose one of the options below or another group that suits your needs.)

  Restore Ministries—*http://www.restoreymce.org*

  Alcoholics Anonymous—*http://www.alcoholics-anonymous.org/*

  Overeaters Anonymous—*http://www.oa.org/index.htm*

  Sexaholics Anonymous—*http://www.saa-recovery.org/*

  Al Anon—*http://www.al-anon.org/*

  Narcotics Anonymous—*http://www.na.org/*

  Other:

- Find individuals to support you.

  (List some individuals below who can support you in your journey.)

  Friend:

  Sponsor:

  Therapist:

  Counselor:

  Doctor:

  Pastor:

  Life Coach:

Personal Trainer:

Nutritionist:

Physical Therapist:

Other:

Step 4—Write a brief description of exactly what your life will be like when this change occurs.

Step 5—Write out a daily prayer to use as you walk the Journey to Freedom.

SAMPLE PERSONAL PLAN OF CHANGE

Self-Assessment: My name is Stan. I am fifty years old. I am twenty pounds overweight and have been inactive since college. Every year I've made New Year's resolutions to lose weight, but I never stick to them. I also have a highly stressful job. I have not been sleeping well, and I know that my eating habits are poor. My alcohol intake has increased over the years, and now I have begun to think about alcohol during the day. When my wife goes to bed, I sometimes sit and drink alone. I'm starting to realize that I haven't thought about having a spiritual life for years. I have become obsessed with the past and the mistakes I've made. I often wake up with a headache and become anxious when I think about going to work. What's wrong with me?

Step 1—Write out your goals.
- *Spirit*—Reconnect with God and build a daily relationship with Him.
- *Mind*—Reduce stress levels and begin to feel a sense of relaxation apart from alcohol. Begin to feel a sense of joy and peace and contentment with life.
- *Body*—Lose twenty pounds by exercising.

Step 2—Take specific steps to meet your goals.
- Spirit—Will get up thirty minutes earlier in the morning and have quiet time reading *My Utmost for His Highest* by Oswald Chambers, and the related Bible verses. Will begin a journal with prayers and thoughts.
- Mind—Will join my friend Bob and attend a Christ-centered twelve-step group at my church.
- Body—Will join a local YMCA and get set up on personal fitness. Will work out four days a week in the morning after my quiet time.

Step 3—Find a support team.
- Support Community—twelve-step group, men's group at church
- Individual Support—Bob; sponsor or accountability partner from twelve-step group; pastor at my church; Steve from office as a workout partner

Step 4—Write a brief description of exactly what your life will be like when this change occurs.
There will be a peacefulness that settles in on my life that is not manufactured through any form of mood-altering drug such as alcohol. I will have a personal relationship with God that is the foundational relationship of everything in my life. I will be a better husband and father. I will enjoy my life and my work, see-

ing it as a part of a greater purpose. Physically, I will have more energy and less stress. Through all of this, I will sleep better, I will feel better, I will look better. I'm looking forward to having a zest for life that has been missing over the past years.

Step 5—Write out a daily prayer to use as you walk the journey to freedom. *Dear God, thank You for this day. Thank You for loving me. I pray that Your love overflows into my life and that my life will abound with hope and joy. Give me the strength and courage to follow through to the best of my ability with this plan for today. Guide me into Your will in all that I do. Amen.*

PERSONAL COMMITMENT TO
THE PLAN OF CHANGE: YOU CAN DO IT!

The first step of our journey together is wrapping up. We've learned how the change process works, how motivation must be intrinsic to produce change, and that the power to overcome rests in a loving relationship with God. We've learned that we can't make it alone. We need others on this journey. We realize that God has a plan for each step of the way, loving us, strengthening us, encouraging us, and doing for us what we cannot do for ourselves.

Now we approach a very critical point on the journey to freedom. Below is a review of what we've learned. Use it as a reference throughout your journey to gauge your growth and to remember the key points of our study together. You may want to review this list each day.

In this journey, you will need a commitment to live by, as well as something that helps you remember your commitment. Below you will find a list of keys for success in your process of change, and a place for you to sign that you are ready to begin your journey. The journey to real change starts with your signature. For accountability, ask a friend or mentor to sign along with you. Ask them to hold you accountable to this commitment. You're on your way to a lifetime of health, hope, and happiness!

KEYS TO THE SUCCESS OF MY PERSONAL PLAN OF CHANGE

- Maintain an attitude of humility and honesty.

- Don't focus on the problems in the past or perfection for the future. Focus on one day at a time and making the right choices.

- Give yourself permission to get started again on your plan if you slip up, but don't stay in that destructive pattern. If you have no commitment to the plan, then admit it and wait to begin until you're ready.

- Treat yourself with compassion. Learn to be gentle with yourself. Don't internalize mistakes with negative self-talk. Go to God. Go to people on your team. Get the support and affirmation that you need to get back on the plan.

- Learn from your mistakes. What are they teaching you? What can you do to avoid these slip-ups in the future? Let your mistakes be a teaching tool, not a condemning device.

- Avoid isolation. Our strengths are in numbers, in staying connected to our team and community. Isolation is a dangerous place. None of us has the strength to make it alone.

- Change is about a process that takes time. Our journeys will take time. Be patient.

- Remember, consistency and time equal change. Take things one day at a time. The new and improved behaviors will eventually come.

- Don't make emotional decisions. Use common sense.

- Don't be discouraged if it seems like you aren't making any progress. So many people quit because they "feel" they're not changing. Don't make any overall decisions about your growth until you are thirty to sixty days into your plan of action. Sometimes it takes three or four tries before our plan finally sticks. Again, just keep showing up. Keep coming back and working the plan. The only way we can suffer defeat is by quitting.

- Remember, in the end, it's all about coming back to God and resting in His strength through His grace. He will take care of you.

Dear God,

I, _____, promise, with Your help and with unwavering determination, to follow through with my plan of change to the best of my ability. God, give me strength and courage. Thank You for Your grace and mercy. May Your love encourage me along the way, and remind me to walk this out one day at a time as I focus on my relationship with You. Amen.

_____

Your Name

_____

Member of Your Freedom Team, Friend, or Spouse

NOTES

Introduction
1. Gerald G. May, *Addiction and Grace* (San Francisco: HarperSanFrancisco, 1991), 42.
2. Luke 14:28–29
3. James O. Prochaska, John C. Norcross, and Carlo C. DiClimente, *Changing for Good* (New York: Avon Books, 1995), 15.

Day 1
1. May, 42.

Day 2
1. Annie Dillard, *The Writing Life* (New York: Perennial, 1990), 105.
2. Henri Nouwen, *Seeds of Hope: A Henri Nouwen Reader* (New York: Image books, 1997), 160.
3. Thomas Merton, *The New Man* (New York: Noonday Press, 1961), 175.
4. May, 42.

Day 3
1. Romans 8:28
2. John 21:5–6
3. Isaiah 43:2

Day 4
1. John Ortberg, *The Life You've Always Wanted* (Grand Rapids, Mich.: Zondervan, 1997), 42.
2. Ibid., 43.
3. May, 73.
4. Martin E. P. Seligman, *Learned Optimism* (New York: Pocket Books, 1998), 48–49.
5. May, 1.

Day 5
1. Genesis 32:28
2. Prochaska, 75.
3. Used by permission from the YMCA *Activating America* campaign.

4. Matthew 11:28

5. Matthew 19:26

Day 6

1. Prochaska, 81.

2. Some items in the list were adapted from Prochaska, 79.

3. Richard Leider, *The Power of Purpose: Creating Meaning in Your Life and Work* (San Francisco: Berrett-Koehler Publishers, Inc., 1997), 36–37.

4. Karen Horney, *Our Inner Conflicts* (New York: W.W. Norton & Company, 1992), 27.

5. Porchaska, 81.

6. Nehemiah 4:3 NIV

Day 7

1. May, 90.

2. Arthur Freeman, Ph.D., and Rose DeWolf, *Woulda, Coulda, Shoulda* (New York: William Morrow, 1989; HarperPerennial, 1990), 106.

3. Seligman, 83.

4. Freeman, 106.

5. Romans 12:2

6. Ibid.

Day 8

1. Thom Rutledge, *Embracing Fear and Finding the Courage to Live Your Life* (San Francisco: HarperSanFrancisco, 2002), 1.

2. See *www.toastmasters.com.*

3. Irvin D. Yalom, *Theory and Practice of Group Psychotherapy* (New York: Basic Books, 1995), 7–8.

4. Prochaska, 111.

5. Http://www.bobparsons.com/Publicspeaking-dowefearthismorethandeathHowIlearnedto dealwithbeingshy.html.

6. Psalm 94:18

7. Jeremiah 29:11

8. Psalm 34:4

Day 9

1. Http://www.eastbayri.com/print/292213007197771.php.

2. Prochaska, 74.

3. Http://cms.psychologytoday.com/articles/index.php?term=pto-20030624-000007.

4. Prochaska, 77.

5. Psalm 139:23

6. Ibid.

7. Psalm 139:124.

Day 10

1. Max Lucado, Sergio Martinez (Illustrator), *You Are Special* (Wheaton, Ill.: Crossway Books, 1997).

Day 11

1. May, 24.
2. Isaiah 1:18
3. May, 19.
4. 2 Corinthians 5:17

Day 12

1. John 14:27
2. Philippians 4:7 KJV

Day 13

1. Proverbs 28:13
2. Charles R. Swindoll, *Come before Winter* (Portland, Ore.: Multnomah Press, 1985), 36–37.

Day 14

1. Prochaska, 79.
2. This is not a blanket endorsement for this type of surgery. There are risks involved. Please consult your doctor.
3. Roger von Oech, *Creative Whack Pack* (Stamford, Conn.: U.S. Games Systems, Inc., Publishers, 1992), card #56.

Day 16

1. Proverbs 22:7
2. Jeremiah 32:27
3. Jeremiah 29:11

Day 17

1. Adapted from Paul Harvey, *Paul Harvey's The Rest of the Story* (New York: Bantam, 1978), 115.
2. See 1 Kings 18:1–40, 19:1–18
3. Hebrews 12:1

Day 18

1. 1 Corinthians 15:33
2. Henry Cloud and John Townsend, *God Will Make a Way* (Nashville: Integrity Publishers, 2002), 153.
3. George Sheehan, M.D., *Personal Best: The Foremost Philosopher of Fitness Shares Techniques and Tactics for Success and Self-Liberation* (New York: Rodale Press, 1992), 10.

4. Cloud and Townsend, 155.

5. Genesis 39:7, 12

6. Prochaska, 95.

7. 1 Corinthians 3:6

Day 19

1. Http://theacc.collegesports.com/sports/m-baskbl/spec-rel/020403aah.html.

2. Prochaska, 48.

3. Of course, we don't want this to become a self-fulfilling prophecy where somewhere in the back of your mind you cause relapse to take place because you believe it's what everyone goes through. You may not. You may be successful on your first attempt.

4. Horney, 111.

5. Lewis Smedes, *Forgive and Forget: Healing the Hurts We Don't Deserve* (San Francisco: HarperSanFrancisco, 1984), 7.

Day 20

1. Os Guinness, *God in the Dark* (Wheaton, Ill.: Crossway Books, 1996), 62.

2. Luke 7:47

3. Hebrews 4:12

4. Matthew 23:27

Day 21

1. Jane Fonda, *My Life So Far* (New York: Random House, 2005).

2. Romans 12:2

3. Fonda.

4. Dr. Harry Emerson Fosdick, *On Being a Real Person* (New York: Harper & Brothers, 1943), 61.

5. Ibid., 63.

Day 22

1. B. B. King, *Blues All Around Me: The Autobiography of B. B. King* (New York: Avon Books, 1996), 146.

2. Dietrich Bonhoeffer, *Prisoner for God: Letters and Papers from Prison* (New York: Macmillan, 1959), 21.

3. King, 146.

4. 2 Timothy 4:6–7

Day 23

1. Jeremiah 29:11

2. Lewis B. Smedes, *How Can It Be All Right When Everything Is All Wrong?* (Colorado Springs: Shaw Publishers, 1999), 186.

3. Ibid., 187.

4. Ibid.

5. W. Paul Jones, "Courage As the Heart of Faith," *Weavings—Woven Together in Love—A Journal of the Christian Spiritual Life*, 13:6.

6. 1 Corinthians 15:19

7. Job 11:18

Day 24

1. Von Oech, card #48.

2. May, 147.

3. Matthew 12:43–45

4. G. Campbell Morgan, *The Parables and Metaphors of Our Lord* (Old Tappan, NJ: Fleming H. Revell, 1943), 41.

5. 2 Corinthians 5:17

Day 25

1. Eileen Spinelli, Paul Yalowitz (Illustrator), *Somebody Loves You, Mr. Hatch* (New York, NY: Simon & Schuster, 1991).

Day 26

1. Rosamund Stone Zander and Benjamin Zander, *Art of Possibility* (New York: Harvard Business Press, 2000; reprint Penguin Books, 2002), 79–80.

2. Freeman and DeWolf, 59.

3. James S. Hewitt, ed., *Illustrations Unlimited* (Wheaton, Ill.: Tyndale, 1988), 226.

4. 1 Peter 2:17

Day 27

1. Philippians 3:13–14

2. 2 Corinthians 5:17

3. Galatians 5:22–23

4. Proverbs 29:18 KJV

Day 28

1. Nehemiah 4:2–3

2. "So we built the wall, and the entire wall was joined together up to half its *height*, for the people had a mind to work." (Neh. 4:6 NKJV).

3. Nehemiah 4:10

4. Rick Warren, *Answers to Life's Difficult Questions* (Wheaton, Ill.: Victor Books, 1985), 67.

5. May, 42.

Day 29

1. Dr. Patrick Carnes, *A Gentle Path through the Twelve Steps* (Center City, Minn.: Hazeldon, 1993), 1.

2. Charles Reynolds Brown, *Finding Ourselves* (New York: Harper & Brothers, 1935), 9.

3. Hebrews 12:1

4. Brown, 11.

Day 30

1. Luke 9:23–24 NIV

Day 31

1. Cloud and Townsend, 52.

2. Matthew 19:26 KJV

3. Romans 8:28

Day 32

1. Matthew 14:27

2. Matthew 14:28–29

3. John Maxwell, *Failing Forward* (Nashville: Thomas Nelson, 2000), 127.

4. Michael P. Green, *Illustrations for Biblical Preaching* (Grand Rapids, Mich.: Baker Books, 1991), 52.

Day 33

1. Green, 264.

2. James 1:2–3 NKJV

3. Leider, 26.

4. James 1:4 NKJV

5. James 5:7–8

6. Kenny Moore, "A Long Run Gets Longer," *Sports Illustrated*, July 22, 1992, 94.

7. Galatians 6:9 NKJV

Day 34

1. Matthew 11:28

2. 1 John 4:18

3. May, 140.

A HISTORY OF YMCA IN AMERICA:
BUILDING, SHARING, NURTURING
FOR 150 YEARS

For 150 years, the YMCA has been a pioneering force in the United States—a force so powerful that, as we begin the twenty-first century, it is arguably the most successful social institution this country has ever known.

The original Young Men's Christian Association started modestly enough —in London in 1844—as a small group of men concerned with serving fellow young men who, like themselves, were new to the city. Twenty-two-year-old George Williams and eleven friends were compelled to help young men find what they felt: God's grace. The first members were evangelical Protestants who prayed and studied the Bible together.

Years later, Boston sea captain and missionary Thomas Valentine Sullivan also worried about the temptations facing young men in cities. Inspired by the work of the first YMCA, he led the formation of the first U.S. YMCA, in Boston, on December 29, 1851.

And the rest, as they say, is history.

One out of three Americans reports being a YMCA member at some point in life, but what's even more remarkable is that the YMCA has touched virtually all Americans in some way. YMCAs invented basketball and volleyball. YMCAs pioneered camping, public libraries, night schools, and teaching English as a second language. YMCAs introduced the world's first indoor pool and group swim lessons. YMCAs offered after-school child care long before "latchkey kids" had been given a name. And YMCAs have provided war relief since the Civil War, aiding millions of soldiers at home and abroad.

In 150 years, YMCA brought about many great organizational programs too—programs it started, nurtured, and shared, such as staff training and certification, which launched the field of professional development. It also established the first retirement fund for any major welfare organization, founded upon a donation from industrialist John D. Rockefeller.

In addition, YMCAs have provided the right environment for ideas and organizations that might never have started without them: The Boy Scouts of America, Camp Fire Girls, the Negro National Baseball League, the Gideons, Toastmasters, the Association for the Study of Negro Life and History, and Father's Day all got their start at YMCAs. YMCA helped found the United Service Organizations (USO), and the Peace Corps was patterned after a YMCA program as well.

The list of accomplishments goes on and on and on.

(Reprinted from YMCA in America, 1851–2001: A History of Accomplishment Over 150 Years, 2000 with permission of YMCA of the USA, 101 N. Wacker Drive, Chicago, IL 60606.)

RESOURCES THAT WILL HELP YOU ON THE JOURNEY TO FREEDOM

Addiction and Grace: Love and Spirituality in the Healing of Addictions by Gerald G. May, M.D.

Changing for Good: A Revolutionary Six-Stage Program for Overcoming Bad Habits and Moving Your Life Potitively Forward by James O. Prochaska, Ph.D., John C. Norcross, Ph.D., and Carlo C. DiClemente, Ph.D.

God Will Make a Way: What to Do When You Don't Know What to Do by Dr. Henry Cloud and Dr. John Townsend.

Personal Best: the Foremost Philosopher of Fitness Shares Techniques and Tactics for Sucess and Self-Liberation by George Sheehan, M.D.

Power to Choose: Twelve Steps to Wholeness by Mike S. O'Neil